THE
MUST-HAVE
CUSTOMER

THE MUST-HAVE CUSTOMER

7 Steps to Winning the Customer You Haven't Got

ROBERT GORDMAN

WITH ARMIN BROTT

T·T

TRUMAN TALLEY BOOKS
ST. MARTIN'S PRESS
NEW YORK

www.stmartins.com

LIBRARY OF CONGRESS CATALOGING-IN-PUBLICATION DATA

Gordman, Robert
    The must-have customer : 7 steps to winning the customer you haven't got / Robert Gordman with Armin Brott.— 1st U.S. ed.
        p. cm.
    ISBN 0-312-35169-0
    EAN 978-0-312-35169-4
    1. Consumer satisfaction. 2. Marketing. I. Brott, Armin. II. Title.

HF5415.335.G67 2005
658.8—dc22

                                                    2005052943

10   9   8   7   6   5   4   3

To my wife, Elly,
who made this book and my incredible life a reality

CONTENTS

CONTENTS

THE MUST-HAVE CUSTOMER

INTRODUCTION

I'm the kind of guy who believes in full disclosure, so I'm going to tell you right now that this is *not* another one of those books about how to make your company great. That's certainly a lofty goal, but like it or not, very few companies are capable of achieving it. For most, becoming "great" isn't even on their radar. In fact, *not a single one* of the "great" companies in Jim Collins's enormously popular book *Good to Great* actually had greatness as a goal. Instead, what businesses really want is to improve, to get a little better every day, every week, and every year. In *The Must-Have Customer,* I'll show you exactly how to do that.

For the past thirty-five years, I've been a very successful business leader and consultant, helping improve the performance and profitability of dozens of companies whose sales range from $10 million to $80 billion.

And over the course of all those years, I learned something remarkable: Companies don't die of natural causes; management kills them. And death doesn't come suddenly; it happens one customer at a time.

If you're thinking that the way to solve this problem is to focus more on retaining customers, you're partly right. Companies die not only from losing great customers, they also die from spending billions of dollars chasing down, acquiring, and trying to serve the *wrong* customers. Those wrong customers not only don't make a contribution to the bottom line, they can throw the entire company off course.

That's the bad news. The good news is that I've got a solution. *The Must-Have Customer* is a simple-to-use tool kit that contains seven powerful steps and a series of questions to ask that have been remarkably successful in helping companies identify and serve the customers who can make the company's goals and aspirations a reality.

Using the seven steps, I guided an international PC company to understand what its Canadian consumers wanted in a computer. The company redesigned its computers to meet these needs and then worked with key retailers on strategy. During the test period, the PC company's largest retailer experienced a 72 percent sales increase.

I assisted a major American appliance manufacturer to improve relationships with its dealers by providing better service through a centralized telesales organization rather than a major road sales force. In the first five years of this new program, sales increased by over 50 percent.

I helped the best plating company in the industry become a full-service business, offering purchasing, machining, polishing, plating, and delivery of completed parts. Now a manufacturer can deal with one company instead of eight to get a finished product. The results? A compounded annual sales growth of over 20 percent for eight consecutive years and profits have grown even faster.

The questions in each step may seem rather basic, but they're not at all simplistic. Together with finely tuned follow-ups, each one penetrates further than the typical, top-of-mind questions managers ask as they attempt to understand their business. Each question yields unique, business-specific insights and information that are the prerequisites for any meaningful action.

Of course, asking the right questions isn't always enough. In fact, a lot of managers regularly pose some of the questions, and most think they know the answers. But those answers are useless—and sometimes even dangerous—if the manager hasn't asked the right people the right question in the right way.

Early in my career, I had the privilege of working with two very smart guys: Jim Posner, the best marketer I have ever met, and the late Don Clifton, CEO of the Gallup Organization. Jim was the first person who taught me that it's the customer, not the company, who makes the rules. Don was a master at testing and validating questions. He taught me how a single word can have a huge influence over the kinds of answers a question will produce, and the misdirection and harm that can come from asking the wrong people the right question, or the right people the wrong question. It's only by knowing *whom* to ask, and *how,* that turns the distractions that limit your company's growth into the objective, fact-based focus that will accelerate it.

Another critical component of the seven steps is the order in which they're used. Each step is carefully designed to build upon the lessons learned in earlier ones. When used in the right sequence, you'll have everything you need to identify your must-have customers, learn their rules, and focus your company on sustained, profitable growth.

In *The Must-Have Customer,* I'll tell you about dozens of companies that took the time to understand their must-have customers, asked (and answered) the questions in each step, and significantly improved their sales and profits. And I'll tell you about dozens of others that didn't do either and suffered the consequences.

Many of the case studies in this book are nationally known businesses with millions or billions of dollars in revenues and profits. However, managers and business owners in *any* business, regardless of size or industry, will be able to harness the power of *The Must-Have Customer*. Even sole proprietors will benefit. Small business owners might not be able to hire high-priced consultants or do the kind of in-depth research that larger businesses can. However, they can still use the seven steps to ask the pertinent questions, then study the answers and make the necessary changes that will increase sales and profits.

The seven steps are not just for sick companies or those that are already in a death spiral. The answers to each step's questions don't produce quick fixes, short-term expense reductions, or esoteric strategic plans that require a nuclear scientist to understand. The procedure is simple: Ask the questions. Put the answers to work. The results will be actionable, practical strategies that management can really use to help even healthy companies grow faster, become stronger, and rise to the next level of success.

Here's a basic overview of the seven steps:

Step 1. Who Are Our Must-Have Customers?
Customers are the lifeblood of your business and

every company has three types. *Core* customers are your company's most loyal customers, the ones who love you and are willing to pay a fair price for your product or service. *Opportunistic* customers see your offerings as commodities and will buy only when the price is right. They generally contribute almost nothing to your bottom line. *Must-have* customers are people who *could* become core customers, but they currently do business with the competition. In Chapter 1, I'll give you the tools to identify all three customer groups and I'll show you how to use this information to steal those all-important must-haves away from the competition.

Step 2. What Is Our Market Position? One of the most basic things companies have to do is know where they're positioned in the marketplace. But the truth is, your core and must-have customers—not management—are the ones who do the actual positioning. Interestingly, in most companies, managers often disagree about where the company is positioned. In Chapter 2, I'll show you how to determine where your core and must-have customers have positioned you, and how to use that information to create a business strategy that will attract more must-have customers while better meeting the needs of core customers.

Step 3. Sweet Spots and Why You Need One. Every company can identify a unique niche, a "sweet spot" where they can win against their strongest competitors. The problem is that most companies don't know where their sweet spot is. In Chapter 3, I'll show you how to study the competition and how to use the research discussed in Chapters 1 and 2 to locate your sweet spot. I'll also show you how to develop a business plan that ensures that your company's sweet spot remains defensible.

Step 4. Why Are Our Satisfied Customers Buying from Our Competition? Most companies talk about trying to satisfy their customers. But satisfying customers isn't enough. In fact, most customers who switch to a competitor were perfectly happy before making their move. In Chapter 4, I'll show you how to go beyond simply satisfying customers and create undying loyalty. I'll talk about the importance of understanding your customers' rules and about doing something most companies find incredibly scary: Fire the customers who are more trouble than they're worth.

Step 5. Critical Success Factors: Do You Know What You Don't Know? In Chapter 5, I'll tell you about the difference between what's *important* for your company and what's *critical.* There's a big difference. I'll show you how to build a strategic plan based on the answers to the questions in Chapters 1 through 4 that will help you focus your efforts on the critical instead of the merely important. This plan will give you the tools you need to develop two or three critical initiatives and outline cohesive goals that everyone in your company can work toward.

Step 6. Must-Have Employees. Having been through the first five chapters of the book, you'll be ready to learn about your most important responsibility: to hire the people who can produce the specific results needed to achieve your company's goals. In Chapter 6, I'll show readers how to carefully select the right people for each position, the people who have the skills and talents to get the job done in the company's unique business environment. Must-have employees know what customers want, which policies and procedures work and which don't, and how the company can cut expenses and improve productivity.

And they'll tell you—if you ask the questions I'll present in this chapter.

Step 7. Are We Communicating Effectively with Our Must-Have Customers? Increased sales don't necessarily translate into increased profits. In Chapter 7, I'll show you how to analyze the effectiveness of your company's communications and advertising, and determine whether the investment you are making is giving you an appropriate return. Advertising that increases a company's share of mind and reach, but doesn't produce measurable bottom-line results should be eliminated. I'll also help you formulate the questions you'll need to ask your must-have customers in order to create more effective advertising.

The Must-Have Audit. Asking the questions presented in the book isn't something you do just once. It's a constantly evolving process, and the must-have audit in Chapter 8 is designed to keep your insights fresh and your company always ahead of the competition. The bottom line is sustained, profitable growth.

STEP 1

Who Are Our
Must-Have Customers?

Customers are the lifeblood of your company. And on any given day, there are two different types of people who patronize your business. *Core* customers are your biggest fans. They love what you do, and they're willing to pay a fair price for it. Best of all, you can count on them to come back again and again. They're the famous 20 percent of your customer base that provides the equally famous 80 percent (or more) of your profits. **Over the long haul, your core customers are the only ones who truly earn their keep—and they're the ones who will guarantee your future success.**

11

Opportunistic customers see your products or services as commodities. They don't care whether they buy it from you or a competitor, and they'll pull out their wallets only when the price is right. They're the infamous 80 percent of customers who collectively contribute 20 percent (or less) of your profits. And you'll spend a disproportionate amount of time and energy taking care of them. In fact, sometimes companies spend so much time and so many resources chasing after and servicing these customers that they wonder why they bother in the first place.

Fortunately, it doesn't have to be that way. In this book, I'll show you a proven process for identifying, attracting—and keeping forever—more of the kind of customer you really want to keep. I should warn you right now, though, that like everything else you do in your business that's important, this process will take a lot of hard work to implement and a serious commitment to maintain. The payback will be continuous growth and sustained profitability. But more on that later.

A Personal Case Study

For many years I was an investor in several Quizno's Classic Subs, a quick-serve restaurant chain. We were a self-service operation that sold better quality food at a higher price than fast-food restaurants. Our competition was every restaurant that sold fast food, such as Blimpie, McDonald's, Wendy's, Subway, and Burger King.

Using comment cards handed out in the restaurants, we continually asked customers to rate our service, quality, and price, and to tell us whether they were regular (*core*) or occasional (*opportunistic*) customers. Our core customers consistently told us that they valued the quality of our food more than price, and they remained consistent and loyal purchasers of our sandwiches. Opportunistic customers told us that they'd come into the store only because we'd been running a promotion—something like a small sub, chips, and a drink for $3.99. During these promotions, we increased our volume by making more sales to opportunistic customers, but our profits actually fell.

And when the promotion was gone, so were the opportunistic customers. Yet our core customers kept coming back.

Tough Decisions

Although you'll never find them on a corporate balance sheet, core customers are a vital asset. The ratio of core customers to non-core customers, and the changes in that ratio, are extremely accurate predictors of a company's success. Companies whose customer base is 80 percent core and 20 percent opportunistic are healthy. They grow organically, increase profits, and thrive. But companies like that are rare. Typically, it's the opposite: 20 percent core and 80 percent opportunistic. For most companies, being on the wrong side of the 80/20 ratio, or seeing their ratio decline over time, is a formula for failure, and there's no other number on the balance sheet that can help. There are, of course, some exceptions: companies that have a very low percentage of core customers and still manage to stay in business. They don't die, but they don't grow, either.

Since you're reading this book, I'm assuming that stagnation and failure aren't business strategies you're interested in pursuing. So what can you do to tilt the core-to-opportunistic ratio in your favor?

First, *don't* bother trying to convert opportunistic customers into core customers. Opportunistic customers are almost exclusively price-driven, so unless your only attribute is low price, trying to chase down opportunistic customers is a waste of time and money.

Second, start subtly encouraging some of your customers to go elsewhere. I know that may sound completely crazy; after all, no one wants to lose customers, right? But the harsh reality is that your business would probably be better off if your customer base were 30 to 50 percent smaller. Now, I'm not talking about making arbitrary cuts—quite the opposite, in fact. I'm talking about eliminating the opportunistic customers I talked about at the beginning of this chapter. Every business has them, and you know exactly who yours are. **They're difficult to work with, drive your customer service people crazy with their demands, buy only when you're having a sale, and account for a large percentage of returns.** Serving these customers gives you a short-term win, but a long-term loss. Keep in mind that the decision to eliminate a customer is a big one and should be considered a last resort. I'll talk more about how to do this a little later in the chapter.

A New Ingredient

Let's get back to the issue of how you go about improving the mix of core-to-non-core customers. Retaining your core customers (more on this in Chapter 4) and getting rid of some opportunistic customers will certainly help, but you can't stop there. The other part of the equation is to get more core customers. And aside from pure chance, the only way to do that is to identify and pursue what I call *must-have customers*.

Must-have customers are *potential* customers who look a lot like your core customers. They're already buying products or services that are very similar to the ones you sell, they're paying similar prices, and the attributes that are important to them are also important to you. These could be quality, customer service, style, low price, advanced technology, or any of dozens of others. In short, must-have customers are the ones you need to be doing business with if you're going to survive. The only problem is that your must-haves are someone else's core customers.

There could be many reasons your must-have customers aren't current customers. They might have had a bad experience with your company sometime in the past. They might not know you exist, or, if they do, they might not be aware that you're selling something they really need. In some cases the problem is your advertising or communications: You're simply not reaching the must-haves with a message that motivates them to try what you've got. (We'll talk about overcoming that problem in Chapter 7.)

Your must-have customers are everywhere—you just have to find them. And if you're planning to stay in business for a while, you'd better get started right now. **At the risk of sounding overly dramatic, your**

company simply cannot survive long-term unless you're constantly finding must-have customers, stealing them away from your competition, and turning them into *your* core customers.

Identifying Your Core and Must-Have Customers

Identifying your core customers is a relatively straightforward process—it's all about shared values. Your core customers value the attributes that make your product or service different. If, for example, your key point of differentiation is that you offer personalized service, that's what your core customers value. If you offer high-quality merchandise, fast delivery, no-questions-asked return policy, a low-fat product, or any of a thousand other factors, that's what's important to your core customers. Without those shared values, your relationship with the customer is purely transactional. You might make a sale every once in a while, but you can't count on any repeat business. Your core customers, on the other hand, have done business with you for a long time. They're loyal, pay a price that provides you with a reasonable profit, are easy (and inexpensive) to deal with, stick with you even after a promotion ends, and pay their bills on time. In short, they're the kind of customer you wish you had more of.

One of my clients, Lincoln Plating, had several hundred industrial customers. And as with most businesses, core customers accounted for about 80 percent of Lincoln's business. Business was okay, but orders and profits had leveled off, and the company was growing slowly. Management spent several frustrating years and a lot of money sending salesmen all over the country trying to rustle up new prospects. But the results were, at best, disappointing.

The plating business is extremely competitive, and given that every new must-have customer is worth between $20 million and $40 million a year, that's not much of a surprise. We knew that before we could help Lincoln Plating attract its must-have customers, we'd need an in-depth understanding of who their core customers were and what made them tick. **The same goes for your business: You can't**

expand your customer base to include your must-haves if you don't know who your core customers are.

If you're running a small business and know all of your customers, it's easy to pick out the core. You already know who your regular customers are and who your big spenders are. You know which ones are recommending you to their friends, and you know which ones you look forward to seeing again and which ones make you cringe when you see them.

But what about businesses that have several million customers? Harrah's, which owns and operates a number of casinos, is a great example. Their Total Rewards program enables Harrah's to track almost every penny Total Rewards members spend at any of their casinos anywhere in the country. They know who their customers are, what they spend their money on, how often they come, how long they stay, how much they bet, and on what. And with all that information, it's not all that hard to come up with a profile of their most profitable customer.

I know, I know, Harrah's has pretty deep pockets. And if spending millions to put together a state-of-the-art customer tracking system is a little out of your league, don't worry. The fact is that if you're using computers, you probably already have most of the data you need. You may not know you've got it, or you may not be using it properly, but it's there. For example, if you're an insurance agent or stockbroker, you undoubtedly have computerized records of your clients' trades and purchases, and it should be fairly easy to identify the customers who make frequent (or at least regular) high-profit transactions. The same is true if your company offers any kind of loyalty program, of if you do a lot of credit card business.

As you'll see throughout this book, I'm a big advocate of solid market research, and the only accurate means of finding out what you want to know is to do it the old-fashioned way: ask. People are remarkably candid and articulate if they know that you're really interested in their answers.

How many core customers do you ask? There's no magic number. The magic—if there is any at all—is in making sure you talk only to the *right* people. When we started this process with Lincoln Plating, they had only a handful of core customers, so we asked all of them. Bottom line, talk to as many core customers as you possibly can.

Below are the questions we asked Lincoln's core customers. Obviously, these work well for a manufacturing company, so you'll need to tweak them a little to get them to make sense for your business. What you're looking for is as much detail as possible about what keeps your core customers coming back.

- Why do you buy from us?
- What was it about your previous suppliers that made you switch to Lincoln Plating?
- What is it about Lincoln Plating that keeps you from taking your business elsewhere?
- What other products or services could we offer that would make it easier to do business with us?
- On a scale of 1 to 5, with one being most important and five being least important, rate the following attributes:
  - Quality of finish
  - Price
  - Turnaround time
  - Material handling

- Availability of personnel
- Responsiveness of personnel
- Information on the status of your order

Once we had a clear picture of our core customers and understood what was driving their loyalty to Lincoln Plating, we knew that our must-haves would need to look pretty similar. So we got on the Internet and put together a preliminary list of two hundred companies that seemed to fit the profile. We were able to determine the products they made, what kind of plating they used, the size of the company, its financial health, plant locations, and in many cases their philosophies about doing business. Then we called each one and asked a few basic questions, such as:

- What types of metal finishes do you use?
- How much do you spend on metal-finishing services?
- Who makes the decision on which supplier to use?

Based on these interviews, we narrowed our original list of two hundred down to about sixty that we felt had the potential to be great long-term customers—companies that were financially stable, would make large purchases, and seemed to value the attributes that Lincoln offered. Companies that didn't use processes Lincoln Plating offered, tended to use low-cost finishes, or were too small were eliminated from the list.

We then brought in one of our best research suppliers to interview these companies. The questions they asked were similar to the ones we'd asked our core customers, but with a twist.

- Why are you buying from your current supplier?
- What made you switch from the previous one?
- What do you like best and least about your current supplier?
- If you weren't using your current supplier, what company would you use instead?
- If you've heard of Lincoln Plating, why aren't you doing business with them?
- What products or services would make Lincoln Plating more attractive to you?
- If Lincoln Plating was able to satisfy your needs, would you switch?

Now, at this point you may be wondering why any company in its right mind would willingly take the time to answer a bunch of questions from someone who was going to try to sell them something. Good question. We simply explained exactly what we were doing and offered each prospect a copy of the completed industry study, which we felt would give them some unique insights into their industry. Naturally, not everyone found that a particularly compelling offer. Some companies indicated that they'd never switch suppliers, and some gave answers that knocked them out of the must-have category. But two-thirds of our prospective must-haves opted in, and in the end, we were able to position our client's services in a way that was specifically tailored to appeal to each prospect's unique hot-button issues.

The results were remarkable. Three of the newly identified must-haves have already become customers. And one in particular has the very real potential to become one of our client's biggest customers.

Of course, not every company has pockets that are deep enough to hire a research firm to help them identify must-have customers. The fact is that you can do something very similar, but on a smaller scale, for almost no money at all. But you'll need to make up for the lower cost by putting in some extra time. It'll take some work to identify your core customers and put together the questions you want to ask them. And it'll take some time to actually do the interviews, analyze the answers, and come up with a profile of the perfect must-have customer. There's no doubt that *any* company that wants to can get the job done.

I can't promise that going through this process will help you land the biggest account your company has ever had. But I can absolutely guarantee that, at the very least, it will give you a clear understanding of what your core customers value about your company, and why your must-have customers do business elsewhere. You'll also quickly find out whether what differentiates you from your competition is actually relevant to your must-have customers. And if it isn't, you'll know what is. That, in turn, will give you the information you need to turn those must-haves into the core customers that will take your business to a new level of sales and profits.

It's critical throughout this process that you ask only the right prospects. If you produce a high-quality product, why waste time talking to people you know buy on price or can't afford your product anyway? Talk only to people or companies you want to do business with. Clearly, the more people you talk to, the better the information you'll have. But, if you only have seven core customers, talk to those seven. Everyone else will give you the wrong information. You'll find even more questions later, in the Digging Deeper: The Fact Finders section of this chapter.

Don't Forget About Your Must-Have Customers' Must-Have Customers

If you're selling to distributors, retailers, or anyone else who will resell or add value to your product, getting them to buy is only the first step. Unless *their* customers make a purchase, your success is far from assured. It's what I call the difference between "sell-in" (making a sale to a middleman) and "sell-through" (when the ultimate consumer makes the purchase).

When I raise this issue with wholesaler clients, they often reply that servicing the ultimate consumer isn't their problem, it's the retailer's job. And they're right—unless they want to stay in business.

Back in 1985, Coca-Cola did a phenomenal job of selling New Coke to distributors—it was one of the biggest new product introductions in history. But within a few weeks, it was clear that consumers didn't like the taste, and New Coke became one of the biggest new product flops in history. The problem was that in doing their market research, they hadn't asked their customers whether they'd buy a new Coke taste. They'd listened only to their distributors—people who had very little to risk since they could return anything that didn't sell.

Fast-forward twenty years, and Coca-Cola is at it again with C2, their new low-carb version of Coke. I'm sure jumping on the Atkins/South Beach bandwagon seemed like a great idea at the time, but if Coke would have asked their core and must-have customers whether they'd buy—and drink—a low-carb version of Coke (instead of Diet Coke, which already has zero carbs), they would have heard a re-sounding no.

Fortunately for Coca-Cola, they've got the re-sources to bounce back from their New Coke and C2 disasters. But most companies aren't that lucky. If you sell your customer a product that just gathers dust on his shelves, it's unlikely that your customer will see you as a must-have supplier. So if you want to stay in control of your destiny, you'd better start understanding what drives the ultimate consumers of your product. The more you know, the more likely it is that you'll be able to give them what they want.

If you're worried that your customer might see you as trying to cut them out of the loop and steal their customers, don't be. Most resellers would be thrilled. And the ones who aren't will change their minds after they realize that you can help them improve their business. Imagine that you're a clothing manufacturer and Target is one of your big accounts. Nothing would make Target happier than you telling them how they can get more people to buy your products at their stores. If you do, you can bet that Target's clothing buyer will be happy to take a look at any new line you bring in. If you don't help Target sell through, that same buyer will be filling up your voice mail with demands to either take your product back or make major concessions on price or terms.

Parlez-Vous Customerese?

As you go through the process of identifying core and must-have customers, it's absolutely critical that you come up with a new language, a way of describing them within your company that everyone will understand. Too often, businesses define their customers—and the must-have customers they'd like to be doing business with—in terms of basic demographics, such as age, income, education, marital status, or any of a dozen other categories. In working with our clients, we've discovered that this is by far the easiest way of segmenting customers. It's also by far the least effective.

Think about the neighborhood where you live. Chances are that most of the houses are roughly the same size and are worth about the same amount. And the people who live there probably all fall into the same basic income bracket. So everyone who lives in your neighborhood fits into the same demographic. Or not.

Take a look at your neighbors' driveways or into their garages. Some of them have the newest, sleekest, most expensive cars, while others have no-frills Chevys, minivans, SUVs, electric/gas hybrids, or antique Model Ts. Some are looking for horsepower and muscle. Others who live right next door and make the same amount of money are looking for fuel efficiency. And some own cars that are worth more than their home. If you owned a BMW dealership, for example, you'd be making a mistake by assuming that everyone who lives in an upscale neighborhood is a potential customer. And you'd be wasting a lot of time and money trying to sell to the minivan or Ferrari crowds.

A far better way of segmenting customers would be to think of them in terms of values or lifestyles. **It's only when you understand those values and lifestyles that you have any chance of turning your must-have customers into core customers.** Now,

I'm not suggesting that you toss out traditional demographics. Gender, age, income, and the rest can be important factors. But they're a lot more valuable when they're used in conjunction with information about values and lifestyles.

Target and Wal-Mart—which attract customers with very different values—are two companies that recognize that a wide variety of shoppers can live in the same zip code. That's why you often see Target and Wal-Mart on opposite corners of the same mall.

In our work with clients, we use a segmentation model that analyzes values and lifestyles in addition to demographics such as income, age, zip code, and gender. While that's incredibly valuable all by itself, this approach frequently identifies more than one group of core customers.

Let's go back to the BMW dealer to see how this works. While there are plenty of BMW owners who make a lot of money, there are a lot more who don't. They're the secretaries or grocery store checkers or young people fresh out of college who don't make much money, but who like the prestige of owning a BMW. More than that, they like the way people look at them as they're driving down the street, they like the way it makes them feel, they think it'll attract people of the opposite sex, or they just like the way it looks parked in the driveway. It's the same story with Harley-Davidson motorcycles. Yes, Harley sells a lot of bikes to big burly guys with lots of tattoos, who drive everyone on the street crazy by taking the mufflers off and revving the engine for ten minutes before they go anywhere. But Harley also sells a lot of bikes to middle-aged executives who are trying to recapture their youth. They won't put a thousand miles on the bike in a year, but they'll take it out of the garage every Sunday and spend a few hours polishing it.

One company that's made an absolute science of this is Best Buy, the largest consumer electronics retailer in the world. Best Buy is extremely picky about where they open new stores. You won't find one on Rodeo Drive in Beverly Hills, or in a heavily industrial area. Instead, they're generally near large malls where there's plenty of parking and lots of people. But even though they locate their stores in particular kinds of neighborhoods, they've recognized that their core customers didn't all fit the same profile.

To maximize the opportunity at each location, Best Buy identified a number of distinct core-customer segments, and developed in-house nicknames for them. Buzz, for example, is a techno geek, a guy who's into the latest and greatest gadgets and who truly understands the technology behind them. Barry is a home theater enthusiast, Jill is the busy suburban mom, and Ray is the longtime Best Buy customer who's into a little of everything. Sometimes Barry and Jill and Ray know exactly what they want; other times they've got a problem they need help with or they need help exploring their options.

Another significant benefit of focusing on values instead of traditional demographics is that you can actually clear up some misunderstandings about who your core and must-have customers really are. When I first started working with Rhodes Furniture, I asked them who their core customers were, and they answered quite confidently that it was women, aged twenty-five to sixty-five, with incomes over $40,000. They were absolutely right. Well, partly. Yes, this group was an important part of Rhodes's business, but those characteristics describe about three quarters of all the women in the U.S. It would have been impossible to come up with a strategy to reach all of those must-have customers.

When we segmented their customers by values and lifestyle, we found that while gender, age, and income were certainly influencing factors, what really drove purchases was the desire to have new furniture. I know, that sounds painfully obvious—doesn't everyone want new furniture?—but coming up with a profile of someone who wants new furniture is a lot harder than it seems. In analyzing the data we collected from core customers, we identified a group that you might call "movers and shakers." They're advancing in their careers and in social status. They have children, aren't afraid to take on some debt, and are motivated to own a bigger home, a new car, and, of course, new furniture. In short, the movers and shakers were Rhodes's core customers.

Based on this new information, Rhodes was able to refocus its merchandise selection with a better must-have customer in mind, and they developed new advertising that clearly resonated with this group.

Playing by the Rules

Another way of looking at this is to imagine that you own a small diner and that you've got one of those No Shirt, No Shoes, No Service signs hanging on the front door. That sign tells prospective customers that you have some rules and that if they don't play by them, they can find somewhere else to eat.

Every company, even yours, has rules. Most aren't aware of them, but by the time you finish analyzing your core customers and prospective must-haves, you'll have a very clear picture of exactly the kind of customer you're looking for. And, perhaps more important, you'll have a clear picture of the kind of customer you'd like to see patronize your competitors. (In Chapter 3, we'll talk about the flip side—the rules that *you* have to play by if you're going to retain and grow your customer base.)

Lincoln Plating's rules, for example, were simple: They wanted to do business only with companies that required technically difficult finishes and valued high-quality workmanship and service over price—

companies like Pella Windows and Harley-Davidson. They also wanted their customers to make large, regular purchases and be financially stable. The whole process of whittling down the number of prospective must-haves from two hundred to sixty to thirty-seven to three was an exercise in identifying prospective customers who wouldn't play by Lincoln's rules and not inviting them to play.

Let me give you one example of a company that has very successfully identified and enforced the rules they have for their customers. Progressive Insurance advertises that if you're looking for insurance, they'll give you quotes from several other insurance companies in addition to theirs. And their commercials feature folks who didn't buy their insurance from Progressive, but who were impressed with the company's honesty in sending them to another insurer. Sounds almost self-sabotaging, doesn't it? But it's very smart. The quote process starts, as it does with most insurance companies, with collecting some basic information about your driving habits, record, age, average annual mileage, marital status, age of your children, and so on. If your answers indicate that you're a good risk, Progressive will give you a quote that the other guys will find hard to beat. But if they don't like your answers, they'll gently steer you toward a less picky competitor by giving you a number of quotes that are far less expensive than theirs. The bottom line is that Progressive will only insure their low-risk, must-have customers.

Harrah's is another company that has some pretty clear rules. Basically, they want people who come to play. Most other casinos try to lure customers with entertainment extravaganzas, fancy restaurants, luxurious hotel rooms, and so on. And those casinos make a big chunk of their money from those nongambling amenities. Harrah's makes its money at the slot machines and blackjack tables. Their core customer is a serious gambler, and the restaurants, entertainment, and rooms are often given free to core customers.

Knowing their core customers so well means that Harrah's knows its must-have customers just as well. They don't waste time or money buying lists of everyone who uses a credit card in Atlantic City or rents a car in Las Vegas. Most of those people aren't interested in Harrah's, and even if they were, Harrah's isn't particularly interested in them. Instead, they focus more on the hard-core gamers. However, with its recent acquisition of Caesars Entertainment, Harrah's will extend its marketing capabilities to a new group of must-have customers who are more interested in nongaming amenities, such as shopping and fine dining.

Businesses aren't the only places where the must-have customer applies. In the 2004 presidential election, John Kerry seemed on the verge of making George W. the second one-term Bush. But Bush's political strategist, Karl Rove, wasn't ready to throw in the towel. He understood that he couldn't get Bush reelected by appealing only to the Republican party's core customers—religious and political conservatives. There simply weren't enough of them. So he set about identifying his must-have customers—people who shared at least some Republican values but didn't consider themselves Republicans—and giving them a reason to make a switch. Many Roman Catholics and Latinos, for example, support social welfare programs, which are traditionally considered a key Democratic value.

But those same groups also tend to be against gay marriage and abortion, values they share with conservative Republicans.

Rove and his team did a huge amount of research—as one party official quoted by the *Washington Post* put it, "They looked at what they read, what they watch, what they spend money on." (I hope you noticed that reading, watching, and spending money are not typical demographic categories.) Once likely Republican converts were identified, Rove created a very focused, relevant message and unleashed over a million Republican volunteers to make the "sale." He didn't waste a penny trying to reach customers he couldn't realistically get. As a result of this meticulously executed strategy, Bush was able to increase his support among a number of groups that the Democrats had pretty much taken for granted: women, Roman Catholics, African Americans, and Latinos. The rest is history.

Do Entrepreneurs Have Must-Have Customers?

If you're starting a business or expanding your current one into a new area, knowing who your must-have customers are and how you're going to reach them is critical. Too often, entrepreneurs have a great idea or product or service and start trying to sell it without a clue as to who's going to buy it. Independent gourmet restaurants (as opposed to franchises of major chains) are a great example of this. They're almost always built around the skills or reputation of a particular chef. The investors or the chef find a great location in a great part of town with lots of nearby parking and set up shop. They spend a ton of money decorating the place and advertising, and a ton of time coming up with a wonderful menu. But they usually spend zero time or money trying to figure out who's going to eat there. It's no small wonder that 80 percent of new restaurants are out of business before their second anniversary. These bankruptcies are often blamed on lack of capital or lack of enough understanding about running a business. Both of those problems can be avoided by knowing your must-have customers, establishing some clear rules about whom you want to do business with, and enforcing them.

A Case Study

As you read this chapter, you might think that the principles behind identifying, attracting, and keeping must-have customers applies exclusively to businesses with hundreds or thousands of employees. Not so. These same principles can be used by small businesses with only a handful of employees, or even sole practitioners such as consultants, stockbrokers, accountants, or attorneys.

A close friend of mine, Rick Grossman, retired a few years ago after a very successful career as an investment broker with Morgan Stanley. Actually "very successful" doesn't do Rick justice. When Rick left Morgan, he was ranked thirtieth out of more than thirteen thousand brokers and had $850 million under his management. That's pretty amazing all by itself, but what makes Rick's story truly unusual is that he did most of this in Canton and Akron, Ohio—not places where one would expect to find one of the top brokers in the country.

Rick started his career in 1966, with Merrill Lynch in Canton, Ohio. At that time there wasn't a lot of competition in the brokerage business in Ohio—largely because no one thought that there were enough prospective investors to compete for. Rick decided that if he was going to succeed in the business, he needed to find wealthy clients. As he put it, "you sure couldn't make a living off poor people." Looking around, he discovered that the folks with the most money (his must-have clients) were doctors. But reaching them wasn't easy—they were too busy to see him.

So he came up with an alternate strategy and targeted people who already had doctors as clients: CPAs, attorneys, and insurance brokers. Rick created some informal partnerships with them and ended up getting an incredible number of referrals. He became the go-to guy for doctors with a lot of money to invest but no time to spend learning how. Rick was glad to take care of them. Within five years, his client base was 70 percent medical professionals, and he was the top producer in his office.

After a while, of course, Rick started to get some competition and he needed to figure out other ways of attracting must-have customers who'd "play by his rules": people with a lot of money but without the time or knowledge to manage it. This time he targeted divorce attorneys—not as clients, but as conduits to clients, in the same way as the insurance brokers and CPAs were. He became friends with a few divorce attorneys and asked them what they told their female clients who'd received million-dollar divorce settlements. The answer was almost always the same: "I tell them to invest it." Rick's follow-up—"Where do you tell them to go?"—led to him landing a number of women with huge bank accounts but who didn't know anything about money.

Throughout his entire thirty-four-plus-year career, Rick never got a client by making a cold call or advertising or putting on a seminar. Instead, he built his business around his must-have customers.

Refining Your Rules

Articulating and enforcing your rules isn't quite as simple as it seems. Broadly speaking, Best Buy's biggest rule is that customers have to be electronics buyers. But that includes just about everyone, so they need a few more rules to get to a more manageable group. Two of those rules are that customers shouldn't be at either extreme of the electronics buyers' continuum. In other words, they aren't interested in customers who are motivated only by price, or looking only for the highest of the high-end equipment. That still leaves an impossibly large group, so we have to go even deeper. What Best Buy is looking for is the kind of customer who appreciates a no-pressure atmosphere (salespeople aren't on commission), high levels of customer service, knowledgeable salespeople, good selection, and fair prices.

As a mass retailer, Best Buy doesn't have a lot of control over who walks into its stores. So how can they—or any other company—ensure that they're spending their resources on customers who will play by the rules? There are a number of options. First, of course, is inventory. By not stocking superexpensive or supercheap merchandise, customers who would be interested in either of those categories don't have much reason to come in. Next is where the stores are located and how they're laid out. A self-service warehouse layout like Costco, with pallets and crates stacked up to the ceiling, attracts a different kind of customer than a store with eager, helpful salespeople who actually know what they're talking about and can help solve your problems.

When Customers Won't Play by the Rules

When customers don't or won't abide by the rules—or decide they're going to pay attention to some but not others—you have three basic options. First, you can change the rules or make new ones. This is essentially what Best Buy did when it identified a number of very different groups of core customers (remember Buzz, Barry, Jill, and Ray?). But if you're considering relaxing your rules, be sure to first test out the idea with your core and must-have customers to make sure you aren't going to alienate them. We'll talk more about how to do this in Chapter 4.

The second approach to dealing with rule breakers is to find out why they're doing what they're doing and correct the problem. In some cases, they don't actually want to break the rules, but you're making it hard not to. If you own a gas station and your restrooms are filthy, you probably won't get a lot of people wanting to spend money in your convenience store. Or maybe you set a bad precedent by taking the old saw, The customer is always right, a little too far and gave into all sorts of unreasonable demands.

For years, the major department stores have been putting too much merchandise on sale and then complaining customers only buy when merchandise is on sale. The Big Three in Detroit continue to produce vehicles based upon production schedules rather than consumer demand, and then they complain that consumers only buy on incentives. Establishing the wrong rules forces undesirable behavior, and look who pays the price: you.

In Best Buy's case, a small but significant number of customers were buying merchandise at free-after-rebate prices, sending in the rebate, and then returning the item, essentially doubling their money. Among lawyers, that kind of thing is called an "attractive nuisance"—like a well without a fence around it. Who's responsible if a child falls in? An open well is too tempting for a child to resist. So is free money from an electronics retailer. In this case, Best Buy changed its rebate and return policies to reduce the temptation. Sure, some customers took their business elsewhere, but others stuck around.

Fire Your Customers

The third approach to dealing with nonconformist customers is to turn them into former customers. I know this is hardly advice that you expect to find in a business book, but the truth is that sometimes you've got to make tough decisions. If a customer isn't a core customer, get rid of him. Again, this is not a step that you should take lightly, and it's an absolute last resort. But sometimes it just has to be done, for the health of the organization. Casinos' pit bosses ban card counters from the blackjack tables, insurance companies are notorious for canceling policies immediately after a claim has been paid, and let's not forget about No Shoes, No Shirt, No Service.

The problem with noncore customers is that they're a distraction. As a good businessperson, you're going to try to do whatever you can to try to serve them. But while you're spending time and money serving your noncore customers, you'll be taking your focus off of your core customers—the people who are most important to your company.

When you're considering eliminating customers, analyze your data carefully and be sure to scrutinize all your customers in the same way. If you ask CEOs who their best customers are, many of them will give you a list of their biggest. In many cases, the biggest are actually the worst. They negotiate big discounts and expedited delivery, demand extra levels of customer service, make all sorts of last-minute changes, and take you away from what you should really be doing.

If you're a small business owner, the thought of losing a customer can be terrifying. Yet in many ways, firing a customer is even more important for small businesses than it is for large ones. As a consultant,

I've learned the hard way that sometimes the fit between me and a client just isn't great. And over the past few years, I've had the painful experience of having to fire two of my largest clients.

Both were great organizations staffed by great people. And I really enjoyed spending time with the CEOs. But as clients, they were impossible to work with. No matter how good my company's work was, and no matter how satisfied the client was, nothing ever changed. We could never get them to move from talking about a strategy to actually implementing one. They were willing to continue to pay us fees, but unwilling to act on our recommendations. The decision to stop working with them was a very tough one, but I know it was the right thing to do. The reason? They refused to play by our rules.

The Gordman Group is very unique in that most of our consultants are C-suite execs who came to us after being extremely successful in their previous careers, successful enough that they don't depend on consulting income to pay all their bills. There's no question that we want to be fairly compensated for the work we do, but helping our clients improve their businesses is more important to us than the money. Our must-have customers are executives who understand that if they want to prosper they'll need to make some changes—and, perhaps more important—they've got to be willing to *make* those changes. The financial rewards of consulting are important, but ultimately, what motivates us is the sense of satisfaction we get from making a difference and helping our clients succeed. So as painful as it might be from a personal relationship point of view, customers who don't play by our rules get shown the door.

Rules vs. Policies

A lot of companies make the mistake of confusing rules with policies. Remember, rules are about shared values. Policies, on the other hand, are arbitrary lines in the sand that as often as not alienate customers. You probably come in contact with idiotic policies every day. The phone company that offers incredible deals for new customers but refuses to give the same deals to existing customers. The department store that insists on making you wait for hours to get a gift wrapped in the gift-wrapping department rather than simply selling you the wrapping paper and letting you do it yourself. The bank that charges monthly service fees when every other bank in town has free checking. The insurance company that denies a claim based on some insignificant loophole. The airline that makes it almost impossible to cash in your miles. The list is endless.

Here's a quick test. Take a close look at some of your policies. If you can't clearly articulate how a given policy benefits either you and/or your core and must-have customers, it's time to dump the policy.

Research: Be Careful What You Ask For

A while back, while on a ski vacation, I received a panicked call from a new client, a national retailer of high-end electronics. He'd just received a critical research report that was supposed to provide the foundation for a new business strategy. But based on the information presented by the research company, my client couldn't identify a single significant opportunity. Unfortunately, the research supplier, a credible national firm, couldn't provide any insights, either. With a board meeting looming in ten days, the client asked me to review the data to see whether I could find anything of value to present to the directors.

The next morning a priority overnight package arrived, and I was shocked to find a six-hundred-page report. The very brief executive summary was bland, didn't say anything of any importance, and I had a suspicion that it had just fallen out of a cookie cutter. The rest of the report was nothing but a data dump. The researchers—who knew nothing about the electronics business—had asked a whole slew of questions to a huge, randomly selected group of consumers. They'd made no effort to understand the answers my client needed or to identify and focus on his must-have customers. But they'd still charged my client a ton of money for six hundred pages of scratch paper in a beautiful leather binder. Poorer and angrier, my client was back to square one.

Clearly we had an emergency situation. Working with my client, we quickly redefined the objectives of the project and hired another research firm that I knew could turn the project around in a week. That new study, which cost half as much as the first one, provided a very clear and detailed understanding of what these must-have customers required to change their electronics shopping habits, and provided the basis for the creation of a new store concept whose results ultimately exceeded all expectations.

Let me give you a few examples of the difference between the first and second projects:

The Initial Project	The Second Project
Asked a randomly selected group of people over 18	Asked only the client's must-have customers, people who had *bought* a piece of high-end electronics within the previous 60 days
Asked consumers where they shopped for electronics	Asked must-have customers specifically where they recently *bought* electronics
Gathered general information on what consumers thought might make them buy a piece of electronics	Gathered specific information on the features and attributes that influenced buyers' *actual purchase* decisions

(*continued*)

The Initial Project	The Second Project
Asked consumers to describe their most recent experience in a store that sold electronics	Asked must-haves about their experiences at specifically named retailers that were our client's *direct competitors*

One Final Thought on Research (for Now)

As the above story illustrates, there's a huge difference between bad research and great research. Bad research yields "nice-to-know" information but nothing relevant that you can act on. Great research is insightful and provides the basis for effective action. Whether you're a huge company with a correspondingly huge market research budget, or a small company with almost no budget, your research must satisfy *both* of the following requirements. If it does, it'll be great. If you fail on either count, you'll have useless trash.

1. You must ask the right people. I can't emphasize enough how important it is to confine your research to your core and must-have customers. Asking anyone else will taint your data and could send your company down the completely wrong—and potentially very dangerous—path. Talking to people who buy $100 boom boxes at Wal-Mart would have yielded very different answers for my client than talking to people who buy individual stereo components for $500 apiece.

2. You must ask the right questions. But in order to formulate the questions, you need to have a good idea of the kind of answers you're looking for. In the case of my electronics client, we ultimately wanted to know where people who purchase high-end electronics are buying now and why. With that as our goal, we were able to structure our research questions in a way that would give us that information. Be sure to ask your "knock-out" questions as early as you can. Getting all the way through your survey, only to find out that the person you've spent the last half hour with isn't a must-have, is a tremendous waste of time and resources.

Focus Groups: Part of the Problem or Part of the Solution?

A lot of times, companies I'm just starting to work with tell me that they've already done some market research and don't feel the need to do any more. Nine times out of ten, when I ask to see their research, they pull out the results of some focus groups they ran. And nine times out of ten, I have to break the news to them that they've wasted their money.

Frankly, focus groups are one of the most misused and overused research tools in the business. Typically, they're made up of small groups of people who are randomly selected and brought together to discuss a topic. Theoretically, the focus group is supposed to provide a good cross-section of the likely consumers that the group's sponsor is trying to reach. Done right (meaning that participants are carefully selected to represent the must-have customers, and the questions are properly written and asked), focus groups can generate powerful insights that can help a company increase sales. But done wrong—which is the way it happens in most cases—the downside risks far out-weigh the possible benefits. Let me tell you why.

First, focus groups should consist only of must-have customers, but they rarely do. Second, one or two aggressive people can dominate the group and drown out others' views. Third, management often sits behind the one-way mirror waiting for the partici-pant to say something that supports the company's ex-isting beliefs. Fourth, since participants are often paid or compensated in some way, they may give answers they think the company wants to hear, hoping they'll get asked back to do even more focus groups. All in all, the information generated is at best, useless, and at worst, misdirecting. "The correlation between stated intent and actual behavior is usually low and nega-tive," writes Gerald Zaltman, a Harvard Business School professor, in his book *How Customers Think.*

A highly respected trade publication I subscribe to recently published a series of articles entitled "Voice of the Customer: Six Steps to Pleasing Baby Boomer Moms." The articles talked about the changes con-sumer goods companies and retailers needed to make in order to satisfy a very important demographic. As an avid reader of fine print—and I've got the bifocals to prove it—I scoured the footnotes for the methodology used to support these important findings. The results? One small focus group done in Atlanta.

The kindest word I can think of to describe that six-article series is "irresponsible." I'm guessing that very few loyal readers of this normally credible publication took the time to investigate whether the findings actually applied to their situation. And I'm also guessing that some of them actually took the articles' advice.

Another drawback to focus groups is that even when they're properly put together, it's easy to reach the wrong conclusions. One client of mine, who works at a national department store chain, hired me to figure out why its sales had dropped significantly two years in a row. I suggested that we conduct focus groups with core customers (whom we could identify from my client's credit card database) in several markets. The goal was that doing the groups would help us formulate questions that we would later include in a valid quantitative study. We set up two groups in each of three cities. One group consisted of credit card customers who had spent 50 percent more with our client than the year before; the other was made up of people who had spent 50 percent *less* over the same period.

In all six groups, there was a definite pattern of purchases being triggered by a major event, such as a wedding or the birth of a baby. This exciting finding opened up a wonderful opportunity to learn about customers' life-cycle events in advance, and then develop appropriate marketing strategies to capture a larger share of these special expenditures.

Unfortunately, one of the company's marketing executives observed one group where an extremely outspoken customer presented a very good case for a loyalty program that would give customers rewards based on their purchases. Coincidentally, the marketing executive had been lobbying for a loyalty program for some time, and this was all he needed to hear. He moved the research-based life-cycle strategy to the back burner and focused the company's energies on the loyalty program. Sadly, that program has never really taken off, and the company's sales remain weak.

The moral of the story is stay away from focus groups, unless you're prepared to do them right, which is a topic so huge that it warrants a book of its own.

Digging Deeper: The Fact Finders

Earlier in this chapter I gave you several short lists of questions that you absolutely must ask in order to identify your core and must-have customers. I worded them fairly generically so they would make sense to readers in a variety of industries. But if you're going to take this information and make it your own, you need to tailor those questions to your own business or industry.

You'll also need to adapt your questions depending on where you are in the process of identifying customers and the kind of research you're doing. If you already know exactly who your core customers are, you can easily ask them what you want to know, and then ask similar questions to your must-have customers. In some situations, though, you'll want to use a blind survey technique, meaning that the people you're talking to don't know which company is asking the questions. Blind survey questions need to be worded generically, but they can be as detailed as you need them to be. Here are some examples of blind survey questions. Again, you'll need to tweak them a little so they work for your company.

- Where do you spend the most for (the name of the product or service)? Why?
- Second most? Why?
- Third most? Why?
- Who is the best supplier of (the name of the product or service)? Why?
- If you could only buy (the name of the product or service) from one supplier, who would you buy from? Why?
- How would you describe the perfect supplier for this product or service?
- What would you require of a new supplier to switch your business?
- What really annoys you about your current supplier?

In some cases, no matter how much you try, you'll have to figure out who your core and must-have customers are by starting with a large, focused group of them and whittling it down bit by bit. Here are the kinds of questions you'll want to ask:

- Where do you spend the most for the products and services we sell? Why?
- Who was your previous supplier? Why did you change?
- If you buy from us now, why?
- If you don't buy from us now, why?

. . . And Never Stop Asking

Once you start asking questions, you can never stop. I always encourage my clients to do ongoing research so they can be aware of any changes in what their core and must-have customers are looking for. I'd suggest you do the same if you can. If you can't, at least make a commitment to doing a yearly in-depth survey.

Now that you know who your must-have customers are, let's move on. In the next chapter, we'll see how your core and must-have customers position you in the market and the direct impact that positioning has on your business success.

STEP 2

What Is Our Market Position?

As Yogi Berra, the great New York Yankees catcher, once said, "You've got to be very careful if you don't know where you're going, because you might not get there." And while I haven't got Yogi's special gift for mangling the English language, I'd add one important—but not quite as witty—thing: "If you don't know where you are, you'll always be there."

So, do you know where your company is right now? Do you know how you got there? Do you know where you're going? These questions may seem silly, but I'm constantly amazed at how few

managers can honestly answer yes to even one, let alone all three. They often *think* they know the answers but they're usually fooling themselves.

The first mistake most managers make is to believe that they control where they're positioned in the market. The reality is that customers and prospective customers are the ones who decide where you're positioned. Actually, you're positioned in a number of places at the same time; it all depends on whom you ask. Some people have positioned you as having products or services that are too basic; others have positioned you as having too many frills. Some position you as not high quality enough, others position you as more quality than they need. Some say your customer service is horrible, while to others it's not worth paying for.

The bad news about all of this is that it can be very confusing. The good news is that you can and should ignore almost all of it. The only opinions you care about are the ones of your core and must-have customers. They're the ones who decide where you are, and they're the ones who decide where you can go. If you don't listen to them, you'll end up in the wrong place or heading in the wrong direction. Let me give you two examples of this.

Back in the 1970s, I was working for a business owned by my uncle in Omaha, Nebraska. The company sold mostly family apparel and home furnishings. My uncle had started the business from nothing and built it into a nice-size company. But around the mid '70s, discount stores started entering our markets, and all of a sudden the future wasn't looking quite so rosy.

In June 1976, I attended a retail marketing conference in New York and sat in on a session presented by a retailer and a marketing strategy consultant named James Posner. The retailer's story was amazingly similar to ours. He'd started a business many years before and had grown it nicely until new competition entered his markets and almost put him out of business. The harder he worked, the worse it got. So he brought in Jim Posner to see if there was a way to stem the bleeding. To make a long story short, Jim helped the company develop a new market position and completely reversed the downward trend.

That was exactly what my company needed! We

flew Jim to Omaha and hired him on the spot. Jim's knowledgeable outsider perspective was valuable in itself. But more important than that, Jim introduced us to the concept of doing market research. That completely changed our decision-making process: from listening to whomever made the most passionate argument, to responding to the needs and rules of the customer.

Our first market research report was ugly. Consumers in our market had no idea what type of store we were. Some thought we were a department store, while others described us as a discount store. Unfortunately, we weren't able to compete in either category, which left consumers just about as confused as we were.

Jim worked with our management team to develop a market position that would provide sustainable growth. Through our research and detailed competitive analysis, we discovered a big gap between these department stores and big discounters. And although we didn't know the terms yet, we had identified our core and must-have customers. We now understood which customers we could continue to serve, which customers we needed, and exactly what to do to take them away from our competition. The results were incredible. Within twelve months, our business turned around and began growing profitably.

The period from 1979 to 1981 was marked by double-digit inflation and record gasoline prices in the United States. They were described as the worst years in the retail industry since World War II. But we flourished. During those three years, we generated compound, comparable-store growth of 17 percent. We were a major force in the regional market and became the company the market was talking about.

On May 7, 2004, Allan Questrom, then CEO of JCPenney, was interviewed by *The Wall Street Journal*. Mr. Questrom was asked, "Shoppers today have so many options, from Wal-Mart to Target to Bloomingdale's. How are you positioning Penney's in this fluid retail climate where consumers are trading both up and down?"

Questrom's answer: "I believe there is a huge moderate market out there, much grander than the upscale market just by the demographics and the income spread. Our challenge is to really become more a part of the customer's life in the income level between $25,000 and $75,000. We also think we can bring people from the higher-income levels in to buy many of the commodities we sell, such as men's and women's underwear and home products."

While one can certainly admire Allan Questrom's ambition, his answer demonstrates a fundamental lack of understanding of where JCPenney was and where it was going. Questrom's goal put Penney in direct competition with every single retailer from Wal-Mart to Bloomingdale's. Penney would have to triple the size of its stores to house the assortment of merchandise it would need to be relevant to such a broad—and contradictory—base of consumers. (I think it's safe to say that your typical Wal-Mart shopper has very little in common with a typical Bloomingdale's shopper.)

When assessing where they are and where they're

going, managers usually make one or more of the following mistakes:

- They ask the wrong people.
- They ask the wrong questions.
- They don't know who their competitors are.

Let's talk about each of these in a little more detail.

THEY ASK THE WRONG PEOPLE

When establishing long-term plans, CEOs and managers usually put together a committee to assess where the company is currently positioned and what the goals are, and to outline a strategy for achieving them. Sounds reasonable, doesn't it? Maybe. But it's a big mistake. Asking people inside your organization produces a lot of speculation based on internal biases, and very few hard facts.

One of my clients, an off-price retailer, believed that his competition was department stores since they both sold a number of the same prominent brands. The difference was that department stores carried full assortments of the current season's merchandise, while my client was only able to get broken assortments of goods late in the season. The CEO believed that the company was attracting the same customers as the department stores because of the overlap in brands. To determine who the competition really was, we did telephone interviews with frequent customers and asked them where they actually purchased merchandise when they didn't buy from this off-price retailer. Much to the CEO's surprise, these customers said they shopped at discount stores that stocked merchandise at price points similar to the off-price retailer rather than department stores with similar brands.

My client believed he was appealing to high-income department store customers, and so the company did its buying and advertising accordingly. But when our research showed that their customer base typically shopped at Wal-Mart and Target, the company restructured its merchandise mix by reducing price points to better meet the buying habits of its core and must-have customers. They also changed the tone and scope of their advertising to better appeal to their target audience. In this case, my client discovered that providing price points the customer wants is better for business than trying to sell prestigious, name-brand labels. Today, this company is extremely successful and growing rapidly. Sales per store and margins have been increasing far faster than the overall industry.

Who's Driving? When It Comes to Positioning, You Can't Agree to Disagree

In many companies, the entire management team is on the same page about where they're positioned—it may turn out to be the wrong page, but at least everyone's there together. In most cases, though, senior decision-makers *don't* agree on where the company is positioned in the marketplace. Worse than that, they don't even know that they don't agree. To help clients sort through all this, I came up with a simple test that I've used many, many times. It's never failed me, and it won't fail you, either.

The first thing to do is to get as many of your managers together as possible. Then, ask them to privately write down the answer to this question: If our company was a car, what kind would it be? After everyone's had a few minutes to think about their answer, ask each manager, one at a time, to read and explain his or her answer.

If everyone picked the same car, or at least the same general type, you're okay—at least for now. You may all be wrong, but you have a better chance if everyone agrees than not. But if everyone picked a different kind of car, you're in trouble. If your advertising people think the company is a sleek sports car, sales picks a stripped-down Chevy, and operations says Rolls-Royce, you obviously have no consensus about how your company is positioned in the marketplace. And if your management's vision is so unclear, there's a pretty good chance that your associates and customers are getting a lot of confusing, mixed messages about your company, too.

This is exactly what happened a few years ago with one of my clients, a Canadian manufacturer of personal computers. The president of the company, a very vocal, dominating kind of guy, described the company as a Cadillac. He felt the company's products, like Cadillac's, were well-designed and top of the line. (Personally, I was surprised at the choice, considering Cadillac's aging demographics and less-than-inspiring design.) The VP of sales and marketing compared the company to a Corvette: fast, flashy, and not always reliable. The VP of operations and distributions picked an Oldsmobile: old, stale, and slow to change.

The car test may seem awfully simple, but don't be fooled. With my PC client, twenty minutes talking about cars led to four days of interesting, often-heated, but critically important discussions. Was the company actually fast or slow, reliable or always in the shop, modern or stodgy? Should the product be designed for industry leadership with cutting-edge technology, or should they go for reliability over speed? How could they reflect all this in their advertising? What was the right distribution channel—distributors, specialty stores, or mass retailers? Given the disparity in the way the various managers saw the company, it took a while to reach an agreement. But once we got there, we were able to create a cohesive strategy to make their PCs attractive to a bigger market. We eliminated some bleeding-edge features, reduced the cost, and backed the PCs with 24/7 customer support. That allowed us to reposition the product as reliable and easy to use. We tested our new strategy with a large retail partner and were more than pleasantly surprised by the 72 percent year-to-year increase in sales to that customer.

I can't emphasize this enough: **If you're not talking to your core and must-have customers, you're wasting your time and money.** Everyone else—including yourself, your board of directors, Wall Street analysts, or other consumers—will give you the wrong answers. **The truth is that your core and must-have customers are the ones who decide where you actually are and where you can potentially go.** Sure, you have some influence, but ultimately, it's the core and must-have customers' votes that count the most.

THEY ASK THE WRONG QUESTIONS

Although I've been talking about the importance of knowing where you are and where you're going as a company, just coming out and asking, "Where are we and where are we going?" isn't going to get you a very helpful answer. As I mentioned above, your internally generated opinions are likely to be wrong, and using those opinions as a basis for strategy could do long-term damage to your company. **The bottom line is this: Your company is where your core and must-have customers have positioned you, and you can go only where they say you can.**

In their book *Positioning: The Battle for Your Mind,* Al Ries and Jack Trout introduce the concept of consumers having a ladder in their mind for every category they participate in. In other words, consumers create their own hierarchy. Department store shoppers' ladder, for example, would probably have Neiman Marcus on the top rung, followed by Nordstrom, Bloomingdale's, Macy's, and JCPenney.

When it comes to making choices, consumers make their decisions based on a set of associations and perceptions they have with a particular brand. In the tissue category, most people would say that Kleenex is high price and high quality, Puffs are a little lower on both, and the generic store brand is very low on both.

In an industrial setting, for example, buyers of goods and services may believe that vendor A has low prices, B has high quality, and C has excellent customer service. And when it comes time to order, they'll go with the vendor that aligns most closely with the factors they're looking for at that particular moment.

It's essential that you ask both groups of customers—core *and* must-haves. In your core customers' minds, you're already doing everything (or almost everything) right, and they'll tell you in great detail why they love your products or services and all the ways you're better than your competition. That's reality.

Your must-have customers, on the other hand, will give you their perceived opinions of your products and services. (Since they don't do business with you yet, they can't give you anything more.) In their minds, you're either doing something wrong or you don't exist.

There are two reasons you might end up in the "doing something wrong" category. First, the must-have customers' contrary perception of your company is incorrect. It could be based on a bad experience they had with you a while back, an article they read, some negative publicity, or even a water-cooler conversation they overheard at the office. Or, second, their perception could be exactly right. They're currently buying exactly what you're selling. But the hitch is that they either don't know that you've got what they want, or you simply haven't given them a reason to make a switch from your competitor.

Whether your must-have customers are familiar with your company or not, you'll have to communicate with them in a way that either establishes an accurate position of you in their mind, or changes the one they already have. We'll talk about some specific ways to do that in Chapter 7, on advertising.

Let's go back to the JCPenney example I used at the beginning of this chapter. If the company intends to pursue Allan Questrom's stated goal of broadening their appeal to just about everyone, JCPenney must-have customers are, well, just about everyone. And that's a problem.

A high-income, must-have customer who currently buys at Nordstrom or Bloomingdale's sees JCPenney as a step or two down, and she wouldn't even come through the door. On the other hand, a lower-income, must-have customer who currently shops at Wal-Mart sees JCPenney as high fashion and probably wouldn't shop there.

At the end of the day, JCPenney must-have customers simply won't allow the company to position itself in either the high-fashion or low-fashion categories. And neither will their core customers. If JCPenney were to try to expand into either (or both) of those areas, their current core customers will jump ship because their need for midrange quality at midrange prices would no longer be met.

You knew I was going to say this, but here goes: The only way to determine where your core and must-have customers have positioned you is to ask them. I'll go over exactly what and how to ask at the end of this chapter.

THEY DON'T KNOW WHO THEIR COMPETITORS ARE

If you've got a pen nearby, you might want to underline the next sentence; it may be one of the most valuable business lessons you'll ever get. **Success in business is not about beating the competition; it's about serving your customers.**

Over the past decade Wal-Mart has been blamed for the untimely deaths of hundreds of small merchants. I disagree. In my view it's really more a question of suicide than murder. The grim reality is that most of these small retailers tried to compete directly with Wal-Mart on price (which no one can do), and killed themselves in the process. The smart retailers—and there are plenty—however, didn't see Wal-Mart as a competitor at all. Instead, they identified a must-have customer who was more interested in quality, service, reliability, or any other factor than price. They repositioned their business to serve those customers in a unique way, and they thrived. Today, retailers wait in line and pay premium rents to be next to a Wal-Mart. Next time you drive by one, see if you can find an empty store in the same shopping center.

Small retailers aren't the only ones who don't know whom they're competing against. Most department store chains, for example, think they're competing only with other department stores. Way too narrow.

My research shows that in consumers' minds—and that's all that really counts—department stores are competing with specialty stores, the Internet, catalogs, power retailers such as Bed, Bath and Beyond, and every other company out there that sells a comparable assortment of apparel, accessories, home furnishings, shoes, or other consumer goods at similar price points. That's a lot of overlooked competitors.

Wal-Mart, however, is *not* a department store competitor. Why? Because it doesn't sell the quality of merchandise that appeals to the department store customer. And not every single store that sells higher-end clothes is a department store competitor, either. **Your potential competition is only the companies that sell comparable products or services at similar prices to those of your must-have customers.**

Some CEOs define their competition too broadly, as every other company in their business universe. Trying to track every move by every company in a similar or related business is incredibly unproductive— and dangerous. It creates a lack of focus that forces people in the organization to look everywhere instead of where the must-have customer is looking. It can also lead to knee-jerk reactions to everything a "competitor" does. And that's a shortcut to business failure.

Remember the "dot-com" boom of the late 1990s? They were masters of technology, the leaders in the new economy, and were going to take over the world. One of the earliest arrivals was Amazon.com, which revolutionized the book business by selling for less than local stores. It didn't take long for competitors to arrive on the scene, boasting that they could sell books cheaper than Amazon, which they did. Unfortunately, Amazon was losing money on every book, and these competitors lost even more.

The big problem was that Amazon's competitors were reacting to what Amazon was doing instead of to the needs of the customer. When Amazon opened fire on Barnes & Noble and Borders, they differentiated themselves by having fulfillment warehouses that could ship single books to individual customers. B&N and Borders had warehouses, too, but they were set up to send out cases or pallets of books, not one volume at a time. Plus, they carried only the most popular titles, not books on dance steps in medieval Mongolia. What Amazon offered was any book—even an obscure one—delivered to the customer's home. Price was a factor, but the primary purchase drivers were convenience and selection. As a result, everyone who tried to compete with Amazon on price alone failed.

Let me give you a few more examples of what happens when companies aren't sure who their competitors are. My Canadian PC client became completely obsessed with the thousands of no-name, store-front computer stores that built unbranded PCs for consumers. Management continuously shopped a cross-section of these stores and then adjusted their prices to match or beat them. The problem was that my client had a massive infrastructure and high overhead and simply couldn't compete with the little guys on price.

To discover who the real competition was, we conducted a national study with the company's own customers. We found that while there was certainly a market for unbranded computers, people who bought them were fairly tech-savvy and not at all interested in paying retail-store prices for my client's internationally recognized brand. On the other hand, core and must-have customers were folks who were uncomfortable with new technology and needed the security of a big-name brand purchased from a big-name retailer. In trying to beat the little guys' prices, my client had hit a pretty bad trifecta: wrong competitor, wrong customer, wrong direction. And the outcome was the wrong financial results.

Ultimate Electronics is a midsize, Denver-based chain of stores that specializes in high-end audio and video equipment. In the early 2000s, business was suffering and management needed to find ways to increase sales. They looked around at other companies that were selling electronics equipment and saw that Best Buy, Circuit City, and other low-cost retailers were selling a lot of CDs and DVDs. So Ultimate started carrying a limited selection of CDs and DVDs, too. When they also noticed that Best Buy, Wal-Mart, and the others were selling a lot of low-end boom boxes, Ultimate started selling low-end boom boxes, too. The result? Business tanked and the company entered Chapter 11.

Ultimate's mistake was not accurately assessing how their core and must-have customers positioned them, and thinking that they were competing with Best Buy, Circuit City, and other low-cost electronics retailers. As a seller of high-end electronics, Ultimate's core and must-have customers were people who probably didn't want what everyone else had. They wanted top-quality, technically advanced merchandise and were willing to pay a hefty premium for it. But when Ultimate started stocking CDs, DVDs, boom boxes, cell phones, and other low-cost products, core and must-have customers walked through the door looking for high quality and found the same basic stuff they could get anywhere. Ultimate wasn't able to attract customers for its lower-cost gear, for two reasons. First, lower-end consumers had already positioned Ultimate as high-end and didn't see them as a place to get basic, no-frills stuff. Second, Ultimate's stores weren't big enough to stock the kind of selection that lower-end consumers could find at Best Buy, Circuit City, etc.

Putting It All Together

How are companies supposed to accurately assess where they're positioned and who their competition really is? Well, the place to start is by asking your core and must-have customers. Before you can do that, though, it's important to be absolutely sure you know who they are. If you don't, you have no way to realistically assess your competition and/or how to respond to them. If you aren't 100 percent sure, go back and review Chapter 1.

You'll get the best information by doing a mix of qualitative and quantitative research with core and must-have customers.

- *Qualitative research* is designed to identify issues that you'll have to quantify later. It should include a mix of focus groups and in-depth individual, reflective interviews. In both cases, the questions are the same. The difference is that in a focus group setting, the questions are put to the group as a whole, while in the individual setting, the interviewer asks a lot of probing follow-ups. As I said in Chapter 1, focus groups can provide useful, actionable information *only* if they are precisely organized and properly structured. Some focus groups should be made up only of your best core customers, and others of carefully selected must-have customers.

- *Quantitative research* consists of asking a larger group of your core and must-have customers meticulously crafted questions designed to produce the information you need to make rational decisions. Most quantitative studies are conducted by telephone, mail, or now the Internet. The questions are created around what you learned in the qualitative phase of the research. For example, if the must-have customers in the small, qualitative study named three specific competitors as alternatives to you, and gave eight different reasons for using those competitors, you can structure a series of questions that will enable you to rank your competitors and tell you which of the eight reasons were most important.

To generate the least-biased results, I prefer to use blind surveys, meaning that the participants don't know who is sponsoring the research. This eliminates the respondents' temptation to tell you what they think you want to hear. Here are some excellent blind survey questions:

- What product or service did you buy?
- Whom did you buy it from?
- Were there other suppliers you could have bought the same product from?
- Who are they?
- Why did you select one supplier over the others?
- If that company didn't have what you were looking for, where would you go next?
- If you wanted a product that was slightly better quality than the one you bought, whom would you go to?
- If you wanted a product that was slightly lower quality than the one you bought, whom would you go to?

The problem with blind surveys is that they have to be fairly general in order to not give away who's asking the questions. In some cases—usually after you've done the blind study—you may want to ask questions that deal specifically with your company and how it rates in the market. You can adapt some of the questions above to focus specifically on your company, or you can create some new ones. Here are a few examples:

- If you buy from us now, why?
- If you don't buy from us now, why?
- If you came to us looking for a particular product or service and we didn't have it, where did you go to get it?
- If you wanted a product with quality slightly better than ours, whom would you go to?
- If you wanted a product with quality slightly less than ours, whom would you go to?
- Which of our competitors are we most like?
- If relevant, how much did you pay?

Once you've done all this research, you've got some important decisions to make. Of course, you make important business decisions every day. But now, since all your data have come from core and must-have customers, you have a far more accurate assessment of where you are in the market, who your competitors are, how you stack up, and why the people you want to be doing business with are buying from someone else—all from the customers' perspective, which is the only perspective that counts.

After doing your research with your core and must-have customers, you'll need to spend some time studying the star performers (as identified by your customers) in your segment of the market. If the research indicated your competition has superior prices, find out exactly what their prices are. If they have better service levels, find out what they actually offer. If it's about quality, buy their product and have it independently tested against yours. Before you start, though, be absolutely sure that you're truly looking at *real* competitors, not just companies that sell similar products or services. Again, if you pay close attention to what your core and must-have customers are saying, they'll keep you on the right track.

Another way to study the competition is to hire an industry-knowledgeable consulting group or a retired industry executive. These people have extensive experience in their field, and they can help you impartially assess the factors that influence competition. It is important to use experts who have extensive industry knowledge rather than newly minted MBAs who don't know what they don't know.

A word of caution. While using industry experts for competitive assessment can give you the benefit of their years of experience, the information you receive is never as objective as facts directly from your core and must-have customers. It's wise to use a combination of industry experts and customer research to provide you with the real story of how the competition is affecting your business.

One more word of caution: Once you've identified your true competitors, don't pay too much attention to them. Sure, a quick look over the shoulder once in a while is a good thing—after all, it's always nice to know what the other guys are up to. But most of the time, you should face forward and stay focused on your own goals and strategies, and on serving your customers.

To match a promotion by a competitor, one of my clients, Rhodes Furniture, started offering its customers zero-interest financing for three years. In talking with individual store managers and actual customers, I discovered that what people wanted was a good selection of furniture that fit their budget and met their basic taste levels. The interest rate they paid wasn't a motivating factor at all. The zero-interest program was actually a negative benefit for my client. It didn't increase sales and they lost hundreds of thousands of dollars in interest revenue.

If you need to make significant changes in your business to make yourself more attractive than the competition, those changes must (a) not alienate your core customers, (b) be relevant to your must-have customers, and (c) provide a measurably superior alternative to what your competitor is offering. Parity isn't enough to make anyone switch. A wonderful example of a superior, customer-relevant alternative is one of FedEx's early slogans, "When it absolutely, positively has to be there overnight." Until then, nothing *ever* had to be anywhere overnight. People actually planned ahead and used regular mail. But that slogan created a multibillion-dollar industry and completely redefined the way business is done.

Invite the Advertising Department to the Last Meeting

I am continually amazed by the number of companies that try to use the advertising department to reposition themselves. Believe me, cases like FedEx are the exception. The rule looks more like Kentucky Fried Chicken.

A few years ago, Kentucky Fried Chicken noticed that people were eating healthier—or at least talking about it—so they decided to reposition themselves as a healthy alternative. While they did make minor changes to the menu, the biggest change by far was their name: KFC. Apparently, they'd assumed that by taking the word "fried" off their buildings, people would see KFC as a healthy place to eat. No one was fooled. Instead, their core and must-have customers didn't see KFC as having fried chicken anymore, and they took their business elsewhere. It took a few years for their customers' message to sink in, but the company recently announced that it was dumping KFC and returning to Kentucky Fried Chicken.

Repositioning Yourself: The Exception to the Rule

Although your core and must-have customers are the ones who decide where you're positioned, you're not completely powerless. It *is* possible to reposition your company.

Kaiser Permanente is the largest nonprofit health plan in the United States. They own their own hospitals, employ their own doctors, operate their own labs, and handle all their own billing. Kaiser got its start in the 1940s, providing prepaid health care for tens of thousands of people building ships in California. For over fifty years—until the mid-to-late 1990s—Kaiser's approach to managing health care was making it hard to get. They thought they could save money by not assigning members a primary care doctor, forcing them to schedule medical appointments two or three weeks in advance, and making them go through layer after layer of "gatekeepers" before being allowed access to specialists. As one Kaiser exec put it, "We chose not to provide our patients with what they desired."

There were several major problems with Kaiser's make-'em-wait strategy. First, it didn't save money at all. Patients who really wanted to see a doctor persisted until they got past the gatekeepers. Most actually ended up with same-day appointments. More important, Kaiser's strategy positioned it as low-cost, low-service, low-quality care.

But starting in about 1998, the company made a concerted effort to reposition itself in the minds of consumers as a "leader in quality and service." To do that, they did exactly the kind of research I'm advocating in this book: They talked with their current core and must-have customers, understood how they were positioned, and learned what the company would have to do to change its image and attract more customers.

It's taken a few years, but today, Kaiser is generally considered a model HMO. Instead of second-tier doctors, it now attracts top-flight health-care providers. Kaiser's core customers are generally very happy with the quality of the health care they get, and its must-have customers now see Kaiser as at least as attractive a choice as BlueCross BlueShield, or some other kind of coverage. The *only* way Kaiser was able to make these changes was by listening to its core and must-have customers.

That's a lesson that the city of Las Vegas learned the hard way. For decades, Las Vegas was famous for its casinos, adult entertainment, and legalized prostitution. No wonder it was called "Sin City." But in the late 80s and early 90s, the city did some market research and got some bad news: Of people across the country who had taken a vacation in the previous 12 months, only 15 percent had been to Las Vegas or even considered going there. By limiting its appeal only to gamblers, Las Vegas was leaving some money on the table. Clearly, they had to broaden their base of core customers.

Casino operators decided to position Las Vegas as a paradise for all tourists, a place people would come for the great restaurants, hotels, shopping, spas, and entertainment. They spent millions building all sorts of non-gambling attractions, including roller coasters, virtual reality rides, and water parks, which would attract young families who liked to travel with their children. All this, including spending millions on advertising, tried to reposition Las Vegas as a travel destination.

A few years and a few hundred million dollars later, the Las Vegas Convention and Visitors Authority and most casino operators realized that the best way to position Las Vegas was to re-embrace the city's roots. (Some, such as Circus Circus and Excalibur, continue to cater to families, but overall, the percentage of Las Vegas visitors under 21 has remained steady at around 10 percent since the early 90s.) They launched a new campaign, "What happens here stays here," which captured the real reason people come to Las Vegas: the fantasy, the opportunity to let loose, to do things you probably wouldn't do at home. This return-to-its-roots approach has been extremely successful. But had the casino operators bothered to talk over their original makeover plans with Las Vegas's core and must-have customers a little earlier, they could have saved themselves a ton of money.

If you're thinking of trying to reposition your company, make sure you don't put yourself in the path of an oncoming freight train. That's exactly what Kmart tried, and they ended up with the largest bankruptcy in U.S. history.

Kmart had been struggling for years, unable to find

a successful formula. To make things worse, the board of directors kept replacing top managers, which meant that the company never had a strategy that lasted very long.

In 2000, they brought in Chuck Conaway as CEO. Chuck was a bright, energetic guy, full of ideas. Unfortunately one of those ideas was to try to "out Wal-Mart" Wal-Mart. Wal-Mart had been extremely successful with an everyday-low-price formula and very limited advertising. Chuck thought the same approach could work for Kmart, so he decided to hit Wal-Mart head on. He cut way back on advertising and lowered the prices of over thirty thousand items.

The problem was that Kmart's core customers were people who loved sales, and they had positioned Kmart as a retailer that gave them exactly what they wanted. They looked forward to seeing Kmart's inserts in the Sunday paper with ads for hundreds of discounted items. But when Kmart went to an everyday-low-price strategy and stopped advertising, they alienated their core customers, the ones who had been keeping the company alive. No core customers = no business. Within four months, Kmart was in Chapter 11.

STEP 3

Sweet Spots and Why You Need One

I'm sure you've heard the story about boiling a frog. Supposedly, if you throw a frog in a pot of boiling water, it'll jump out right away. But if you put it in a pot of cool water and slowly increase the heat, the frog won't notice the threat until it's too late. In a sense, your company's positioning is like that frog and your market is the water. Getting too comfortable with your positioning often leads to complacency, and complacency can lead to death. Remember Fuller Brush and Smith Corona? How about these discount chains: Ames, Bradlees, Caldor, Jamesway, Venture, White

Front, Turnstyle, and Grants? The world kept changing around them, but they ignored it and kept right on doing business the way they always had—all the way into bankruptcy.

So what's the solution? **Your company will thrive over the long haul only if you're able to leverage your strengths to create a customer-relevant position in the marketplace.** Put a little more succinctly, you've got to create a "sweet spot" that your competitors can't touch. Creating that spot will enable you to successfully compete—and win—against the strongest competition. Your sweet spot is what will move your company from average or below average to industry leader.

With all the talk these days about "niche marketing," it's tempting to assume that "niche" and "sweet spot" are interchangeable terms. Don't. There's a big difference. A niche is a place you go, a perceived opening in the marketplace. A sweet spot is taking that niche and creating an impenetrable fortress. Every element of your business is crafted to capture the heart and mind of a specific group of customers.

If you don't have a sweet spot, every day is like swimming in quicksand. No matter how much you flail around, you can't keep yourself from sinking. It's infuriating, frustrating, not to mention life-threatening. Running a business without knowing your sweet spot is never fun. Increasing your earnings is a constant struggle, and margins erode rather than grow. You're always looking for ways to cut expenses, and investing in the future of your business takes a backseat to simply surviving.

With a sweet spot, however, it's a very different story. You know your strengths and you have a clear vision of where your company can realistically go. You're no longer in direct competition with your industry rivals. In fact, you've created a new industry. Your must-have customers become loyal, core customers, operations run smoothly, margins are healthy, and sales grow. Don't believe me? Try to think of a successful company that doesn't have a sweet spot, something they do better than anyone else.

The list is endless: Think of Amazon, eBay, Coca-Cola, McDonald's, Nordstrom, Southwest Airlines. They all do something better than anyone else. Ritz-Carlton's sweet spot is catering to wealthy executives, while Marriott's Courtyard chain takes care of the other end of the spectrum: cost-conscious business travelers. The Body Shop, which sells cosmetics, created a sweet spot by offering "beauty without cruelty"—environmentally friendly products that aren't tested on animals. And Domino's sweet spot was offering "fresh, hot pizza delivered in thirty minutes or less, guaranteed" (although in many markets they've changed it to forty-five minutes because too many of their drivers were getting into accidents trying to beat the thirty-minute clock).

Let me give you a more detailed example from one of my favorite clients, Lincoln Plating. The most enjoyable and satisfying experience of my fourteen years in consulting has been working with Lincoln's CEO, Marc LeBaron, who transformed his company from a small, regional commodity metal finisher in a minor midwestern market into the industry leader. Marc is one of those rare, insightful managers who has a never-ending need for facts. Through ongoing research with must-have customers, he identified a unique sweet spot and built an entire organization around it.

Clients use Lincoln Plating and its integrated processing for high-quality, completed assemblies, delivered on time, and ready for mounting on their company's main products. Lincoln Plating associates design a part so it can be cost-effectively manufactured, efficiently plated, and delivered in the quantities the manufacturer needs, exactly when the manufacturer needs it. Does Lincoln Plating charge a fair price for its services? Absolutely, but the company saves its clients money every time. Doubt that companies will work with a premium supplier when they can get the product cheaper from someone else? Just ask Harley-Davidson or Pella Windows, two of their largest clients, why they rely on Lincoln Plating for high-quality manufactured and plated parts.

GEICO Insurance is another great example. There are literally hundreds of companies out there that sell auto insurance, and most offer similar policies at similar prices. In that kind of market it's easy to get lost. But GEICO carved out a sweet spot by targeting only very low-risk drivers, people who most likely won't ever need insurance. Since their exposure is limited, GEICO can charge very competitive prices and still generate a superior profit. Their growth rate exceeds the rest of the industry's and has for quite some time. In fact, GEICO's sweet spot is so desirable that Warren Buffett bought the company.

When I talk with clients about creating a sweet spot, this is often where they stop me. "Competition is too fierce in our industry," they say. "It's impossible to find a sweet spot in that kind of market." I'll tell you the same thing I tell them: It's a basic law of physics that two objects can't occupy the exact same space at the same time. The same applies to business. **There is *always* a way to find a sweet spot, no matter how saturated your category. If you can't find it, you're not looking hard enough.** Let me give you a few examples.

Take Dell Computers. Just a decade ago, Dell was able to leverage its strengths—a low-cost operation and an unerring sense of what its must-have customers want—to become the world's number one direct seller of personal computers to businesses and individuals. While Dell consistently trounces the competition, about fifteen thousand smaller PC manufacturers in the U.S. alone have carved out profitable sweet spots for themselves. Some are local companies that make customized white-box PCs for low-end home and business use. Others are highly specialized, like Alienware Corporation, which designs and manufactures high-performance computers for gaming, home entertainment, and personal use.

The grocery business is one of the most crowded and competitive categories out there. Nevertheless, that hasn't done much to slow down Whole Foods. The company, which is now the world's largest retailer of natural and organic foods, got its start in the tofu and bean sprouts era of the 1970s. But it's more than a purveyor of free-range chicken and organically grown produce. Whole Foods offers a superior selection of high-quality food and attentive customer service in an upscale, inviting, easy-to-shop environment. Bread and pastries are baked fresh twice a day. A wide selection of antibiotic- and hormone-free fresh seafood, chicken, and meat are displayed on beds of crushed ice. And the prepared food section is crammed with appetizing entrees, vegetables, potatoes, and salads. Areas such as the meat department are staffed out front with knowledgeable, helpful people.

Go into a Whole Foods market anywhere in the

country and you'll find that the aisles are filled with shoppers, no matter the time of day. At lunchtime people are stacked two and three deep in front of the prepared food section looking for a tasty alternative to fast food. At the Whole Foods in Denver, I often buy roasted, unsalted cashews without thinking twice about paying the price since this is one of the few places that sells them.

Whole Foods is clearly not just another grocery store. The entire business is built around satisfying the needs of a very specific kind of customer, one for whom low price is not a priority. That sweet spot elevates it above the commodity grocery stores that offer a broad assortment of consumables but limited customer service. The company's financials show just how successful a sweet spot can be: Comparable store sales for the 2004 fiscal year were up 14.9 percent—a company record. During the same period, Kroger (one of the country's largest grocery chains) had comp store sales that were up only 1.2 percent. Whole Foods' gross margin was 34.7 percent in 2004, while Kroger's was 25.4 percent.

The casino business is also incredibly competitive,

but that hasn't stopped Harrah's from carving out a very profitable sweet spot serving people who are more interested in making bets and getting outstanding service than in getting a good seat for the show. Their hotel occupancy rates are north of 90 percent year-round. Compare that to the industry average of about 60 percent, and a Las Vegas average of about 80 percent.

Sometimes an imaginative entrepreneur can create an entirely new industry and then dominate the sweet spot position. Remember the twenty-five-cent cup of joe? You used to be able to get a no-frills cup of coffee in restaurants, convenience food stores, gas stations, and even the occasional independently owned coffeehouse. Then along came Howard Schultz, CEO of Starbucks, who brought the European coffee bar culture and lifestyle to the United States. Before Starbucks, coffee was just a low-priced commodity. Now it's a lifestyle choice.

Schultz didn't just open coffeehouses, which he knew would be too easy to copy and would eventually turn into a commodity. Instead, he created a sweet spot that he describes as "the third place." The first place is home, second is work, and Starbucks is the place you want to be when you're not at the other two.

Pass by a Starbucks any time of day and look in the window. Almost every table is in use and people are lined up waiting to order. Over the years Schultz's vision has grown, and today Starbucks has over eight thousand locations worldwide. In some metropolitan cities it seems as if there is a Starbucks on every corner. In Frisco, Colorado, near my home, there is a full-line Starbucks on one corner and a smaller Starbucks Express in the Safeway grocery store two blocks down the street.

Even when an industry is dominated by one or two companies, it's still quite possible for others to carve out profitable sweet spots that keep them from going belly-up from seemingly overwhelming competition. Take Kmart, for example, which was once the dominant chain in the discount segment. Then along came Sam Walton who put his Ben Franklin variety stores on the line and opened the first Wal-Mart, in Rogers, Arkansas. Over the next twenty-five years, Wal-Mart carved out a sweet spot: a low-margin, high-volume "distribution company" business that meets customers' needs with selection and low prices. Today, Wal-Mart is the largest company in the world, while Kmart is still struggling to define its own sweet spot in the marketplace.

In the previous chapter, I talked about how small retailers were competing successfully against Wal-Mart. Large retailers have done just as well—provided they had a sweet spot. Target, for example, has created its sweet spot by offering more upscale merchandise at slightly higher prices than Wal-Mart—exactly what its must-have customers want.

If you think that Target is an exception, you might want to take a look at the annual reports of Walgreens, Tractor Supply, Dollar General, and Costco. These four retailers also sell products similar to those sold at Wal-Mart, but have identified different consumer-relevant sweet spots. Walgreen's has a higher cost of doing business than Wal-Mart or Target, but it produces comparable financial results. The company's sweet spot is that it offers customers convenience and superior selection in the health and beauty care categories, but not always at the lowest price. New Walgreens stores have drive-through pickup windows for prescriptions, a time-saver for busy people and handy for sick people who don't want to drag themselves out of their cars. Walgreen's has about two hundred less stores than its closest rival CVS, but does over $2 billion more in sales.

Tractor Supply, with 433 stores in thirty states, is the largest retail farm and ranch store chain in the United States. Its core and must-have customers are full-time farmers, horse owners, ranchers, part-time and hobby farmers, suburban and rural homeowners, contractors and tradespeople. Stores are located in rural areas and on the outskirts of large cities. The shelves are lined with products that customers need to work their farms, ranches, or home property. There is some overlap with Wal-Mart in items such as pet supplies and lawn, garden and maintenance supplies. But most of the products, like fence-building materials, tractor/trailer parts, and welding and pump supplies, are not found in Wal-Mart stores. So it's good news for Tractor Supply when Wal-Mart builds a store nearby and increases the retail traffic in the area.

The happiest day for these companies is when Wal-Mart announces it is coming to a location near one of their stores. Wal-Mart brings customers to the area who many times are looking for products that can only be purchased from these other retail chains.

Another way to dominate a sweet spot is to change an industry paradigm. Intuit, the maker of Quick-Books, Quicken, and TurboTax, wasn't the first company to offer personal and business finance programs. However, cofounder Scott Cook was committed to producing a truly user-friendly financial software. He set the standard by doing constant customer research and asking for feedback. Intuit's commitment to this sweet spot was so strong that they actually followed new purchasers home (with their permission, of course) and watched them install and use the software. The result has been a suite of financial products that outperform every other industry competitor—even Microsoft's Money.

Let me give you one last example of how a company of almost any size can capture a sweet spot against the competition. In January 1966, I bought an engagement ring for my future wife from Borsheim's, a small jewelry store in downtown Omaha, Nebraska. Back then, everyone in Omaha knew that Borsheim's was *the* place to go for good prices on fine jewelry, watches, sterling silver, and fine china.

Fast-forward forty years. Borsheim's, now owned by Warren Buffett's Berkshire Hathaway and operating in a fifty-thousand-square-foot store in a prestigious shopping center, draws 45 percent of its sales volume from forty-nine states and five continents. How? By attracting its must-have customers with an unwavering, decades-long commitment to offering a selection of merchandise unlike that found in most other jewelry stores. The company has positioned itself as a seller of premium jewelry and gifts at prices usually 25 percent to 33 percent less than manufacturer's suggested retail.

Borsheim's isn't a household name like Tiffany's. However, that hasn't kept it from becoming the second-largest jewelry store in the country in terms of merchandise sold from a single location. Only Tiffany's Fifth Avenue store in New York, with annual sales close to $220 million, sells more merchandise.

(Oh, and did I mention that Borsheim's is where Bill Gates purchased his wife's engagement ring? I think it's nice to have something in common with the world's richest man.)

Creating Your Own Sweet Spot

I've given you plenty of examples of how successful companies used sweet spots to grow their businesses. Yes, most of the examples are companies that are much larger than yours. But don't worry. **A company *can* definitely flourish even if it's run by mere mortals. The only requirement is that management must have a clear vision of where the company can go based on a rational analysis of where its core and must-have customers will *permit* it to go.**

An online dating service, for example, might serve only single parents, the over-sixty set, or people of a particular religion. A local pet store might specialize in exotic birds or sell organic cat food. Your neighborhood butcher might have the best prices on Japanese beer-fed, Kobe beef. A toy store might sell only antique-style toys made in the Ozark Mountains. A real-estate agent might decide to target first-time home buyers, the elderly, or historic properties, or châteaux on the Riviera. You get the point.

Even a sole proprietor can have a sweet spot. My coauthor, for example, created a sweet spot by writing books that provide advice and support to expectant and new fathers. And in my business, I created a sweet spot in a very crowded consulting industry by employing only former senior executives with a track record of superior results. We never send out a new MBA for our clients to train.

One of my favorite small-business sweet spot examples is my friend Rick Grossman, the very successful stockbroker you met in Chapter 1. Rick's sweet spot was people who had a lot of money but no time to manage it. When Rick was first starting out, there wasn't a lot of competition. Then, after a few years, other brokers came into the market and started chasing after the same clients. So Rick tweaked his sweet spot a little. He'd seen a survey done by the New York Stock Exchange about why stockbrokers lost clients. The number one answer by far was "neglect."

Rick began to insist on meeting each of his clients at least once every quarter. It didn't matter to Rick whether it was a 6:00 A.M. breakfast or a 6:00 P.M. chat after work. He sat down face-to-face with his clients and he told them exactly what was happening with their portfolios. The meetings were usually pretty short because most of his clients really didn't know much about investing and didn't want to know. What they cared about was that someone was looking out for them. Their CPA or their attorney would have billed them a hefty hourly rate to get together, and their insurance broker would have tried to sell them something. But Rick never charged his clients, and eventually, they'd build up a close relationship. He lost a client now and then, usually when a client's brother-in-law became a broker or something like that. However, over the course of his whole career, he never lost one due to neglect. That's a sweet spot very few companies of any size can touch.

Finding Your Sweet Spot

Whatever the size of your company, your first order of business is to take off your rose-colored glasses and honestly analyze the realities of your market. And while you're at it, if you've got an "I can beat anyone" attitude, get rid of it. If you're lucky, you already know what your sweet spot can be. Your must-have customers may have pointed out one or two specific aspects of your business (products, services, or anything else) that they love. Or, after studying the competition you've discovered a niche that hasn't been fully developed by anyone else.

If you're not that lucky, you'll need to do some research by asking your core and must-have customers the following questions. The answers will give you some clear, objective ideas for how to tweak your company positioning to create and dominate a unique and profitable sweet spot.

- Where do you purchase the items or services we sell today? Why do you purchase from that supplier?
- How long have you used this supplier?
- What do you like best about this supplier?
- What don't you like about this supplier?
- If this company did not exist, who would you go to? Why?
- If another supplier offered something similar for 10 percent less, would you switch?
- How about 20 percent? Or 30 percent?
- If you could create the perfect supplier for you, what would it be like?

As you'll soon find out for yourself, one of the great things about sweet spots is that they act as a kind of business risk insurance. Whenever the economy—or even a single category—turns downward, the company with the sweet spot suffers much less than everyone else. When retail tanks, Wal-Mart almost always comes out unscathed. Right after 9-11, Walgreens continued to grow on a same-store basis, while CVS faltered. And when the computer business took a turn for the worse, Dell hardly noticed, HP and Gateway had serious trouble, and IBM got out of the PC business altogether.

Can You Have Multiple Sweet Spots?

In an earlier chapter I talked about JCPenney making the colossal mistake of adopting a strategy of LBOE (a little bit of everything), and trying to be all things to all customers. **Done right, though, it's quite possible to have multiple sweet spots and multiple groups of core and must-have customers. You just can't do it in the same place.**

Many of the major hotel chains have identified a spectrum of sweet spots that appeal to must-have customers with different needs. Take Marriott, for example, which since 1957 has grown from one hotel in Arlington, Virginia, to a worldwide chain of eleven brands in the United States and sixty-four other countries and territories. The company's 2,200 hotels include full-service hotels and resorts, moderately priced hotels, extended-stay hotels, midpriced extended-stay hotels, consistent, quality hotels at affordable prices, moderately priced, all-suite hotels, and high-end elegant, luxurious hotels. Marriott knows how to maximize its business model by providing lodging options to a variety of must-have customers.

In the grocery business, most chains concentrate on a single niche, such as full-service with delis, floral shops, and pharmacies, or low-cost, no-service box stores. Loblaw, the largest and most profitable food retailer in Canada, has a portfolio approach to selling groceries. As they put it, "Loblaw is committed to providing Canadians with a one-stop destination in meeting their food and everyday household needs."

The company has four distinct—and highly successful—sweet spots in the market place: no-frills, conventional supermarkets, superstores, and combination stores. Breaking with grocery tradition, Loblaw owns most of its own corporate stores. This gives the company the flexibility to make changes in store formats to meet changing customer needs. Loblaw operates on the principle of market share per store rather than share of sales per market. As Dick Currie, president of Loblaw, said in a 2000 Harvard Business School case study, "When we see a hole in the market, we see about filling it."

One of Loblaw's strengths has been the development of private label brands that set it apart from the competition. In 1984, Loblaw introduced its President's Choice line: superior-quality products sold at the same price as the national brands. Before President's Choice, the term "private label" was nearly synonymous with "lowest-priced, lowest-quality product on the shelf." Today, Loblaw sells five thousand different President's Choice products. Its other private-label brands include 'Too Good to Be True,' (nutritionally enhanced food products), environmentally friendly G*R*E*E*N products, and Club Pack (large packages sold at warehouse prices).

Three Final Warnings

The sweet spot concept is very powerful, but building one has to be done very carefully. Oftentimes, companies are in such a hurry to create a sweet spot that they fall into one of the following traps. I've seen it over and over and over. Hopefully, after reading this section, you won't make the same mistakes.

- **Learn how to say no.** The greatest enemy of creating a sweet spot is the "no problem, we can do that" mentality. Lots of entrepreneurs, especially those who are just starting out, don't like to say no to an order. So when a customer asks for something that's out of the sweet spot range, the entrepreneur does everything he can to give the customer what he wants. Now, all of a sudden, the company finds itself doing dozens of things for the first time, reinventing the wheel over and over again. It no longer benefits from the value and efficiencies that knowledge and experience bring. While satisfying your customers is generally an excellent idea, if it ends up getting in the way of your laser-like focus on your sweet spot, it'll end up costing you your competitive advantage. Saying "no, we can't do that" every once in a while can actually help your business succeed.
- **Don't be a copycat.** The worst possible strategy is to attempt to duplicate the success of the industry

leader. Remember the story I told in Chapter 2 about Kmart trying to duke it out with Wal-Mart? Unfortunately, then-CEO Chuck Conaway saw Wal-Mart as a model for where he wanted to go with Kmart. He didn't conduct any relevant customer research to determine the needs of the company's must-have customers. As a result, he couldn't determine a viable sweet spot that would have kept Kmart from slamming up against the Wal-Mart fortress and ending up in bankruptcy court.

- **Be realistic.** While many business attributes can be changed with time, patience, and money, some are almost impossible. A high-cost company, for example, can't easily become a low-cost one. Again, think about Kmart, which made the mistake of going toe-to-toe with Wal-Mart. It took the country's largest bankruptcy to force the company to make the transition to a leaner organization. A bureaucratic company can't easily become quick and agile. Not sure that's true? Ask IBM about the PC business. Their bureaucracy was so entrenched that it effectively killed their ability to stay current and cost-effective in a fast-changing market. A process-driven company can't easily become fertile ground for creativity. Want proof? Sam's

Club is the warehouse division of Wal-Mart, the world's largest retailer. Management of this division is focused only on low price. The creative merchants at Costco, a competing warehouse company, continuously generate double the volume per store of Sam's Club. Why? The management at Costco is focused on offering its customers a continuously changing selection of more interesting merchandise.

As we've discussed in this chapter, the magic for a company happens when management matches the realities of the business with a meaningful customer-relevant sweet spot in the market. Next, you need to understand what you have to do to retain your current customers and attract new customers from your competitors. A profitable business must develop intense customer loyalty. In the next chapter, we'll talk about what you'll need to do to get—and keep—customers who are satisfied and loyal.

STEP 4

Why Are Our Satisfied Customers Buying from Our Competition?

If your company isn't as successful as it could be, it may be because you're satisfying your customers. Yes, you read that correctly. Having a satisfied customer base could be the worst thing to happen to your business.

Okay, now that the provocative chapter opening is out of the way, let me explain.

When you're satisfying your customers, you're simply meeting their expectations and not doing anything major to drive them away. You're also not doing anything to make them want to come back again. As a result, most won't. According to research conducted by Bain & Company, a global management consulting firm, 65 to 85 percent of customers who defect to a competitor say they were "satisfied" or "very satisfied" just before they made their move. All in all, customers who say they're satisfied are almost as likely to change suppliers as those who say they're unsatisfied. **Put another way, a satisfied customer is a former customer waiting to happen.**

So if customer satisfaction isn't the goal, what is? In a word, *loyalty.* Satisfied customers have no particular attachment to your company or your brand and it doesn't take much to get them to move. One strike and you're out. In fact, satisfied customers buy from the competition all the time. If you want proof, just look in the mirror. How many times have you been perfectly happy with a particular product or service but taken your business to a competitor? Studies have found that only 9 percent of defecting customers left because of the competition, and only 14 percent because their former supplier didn't properly address their concerns. More than two thirds—68 percent—didn't have a specific reason. Loyalty, on the other hand, buys you forgiveness. Loyal customers will stick by you. They'll brave a little inconvenience to do business with you, and they'll forgive your mistakes (up to a point). They're committed to getting the products or services you offer from you alone and it'll take something truly earth-shattering to get them to go elsewhere. Bottom line? **Satisfaction is temporary. Loyalty can be forever.**

Unfortunately, too many companies make the mistake of using the terms "satisfaction" and "loyalty" interchangeably. Bain & Company reports that 90 percent of car owners say they're satisfied with their current car. That's a figure that most auto manufacturers are delighted to hear. The problem is that only 40 percent of those satisfied customers buy their next car from the same manufacturer. Lexus, on the other hand, is far more interested in customer loyalty, which they define as "subsequent purchases by previous buyers." They enjoy a retention rate of over 60 percent—lower than what they'd like to have but 50 percent better than the industry average.

Turning Satisfaction into Loyalty:
You've Got to Know the Rules

At this point you may be wondering how one goes about turning satisfied customers into loyal ones. Well, simply put, it's all about the rules. Remember the No Shirt, No Shoes, No Service signs we talked about back in Chapter 1? Those were *your* rules, the specific traits that your company looks for in a customer. Anyone who doesn't have those traits—in other words, who doesn't play by your rules—well, let's just say you'd prefer that they patronize one of your competitors.

Whether you know it or not, customers have rules, too. You do, I do, and so does everyone you do business with. Customers' rules are the policies, beliefs, desires, expectations, and needs that together determine how, when, what, and why they buy. Take a second and think about some of your own rules and how they determine your shopping and purchasing decisions. While you're doing that, let me tell you about a few of my rules.

Since I travel forty weeks a year, a lightweight computer is very important to me. So I have a simple rule about computers: If it weights over four pounds, I don't buy it. I don't care about the technology. I don't care about the quality of the screen. I don't care about bits and bytes. I don't even care about the brand. The only rule I have is that it can't be over four pounds, and nothing else counts.

My wife and I recently built a home, and we have dozens of floodlights in the ceilings. Before building the house, I was a loyal GE lightbulb customer, it's the only brand I've ever trusted or bought. But their floodlights have a big GE logo right on the face, which turned my ceilings into GE billboards. As much as I like GE, I hate the way their logo makes my ceilings look, so I made a new rule: If a bulb has a label on the face, I won't buy it. GE didn't feel like playing by my rule, but Phillips did. Now I'm a loyal Phillips lightbulb customer.

Now, while everyone has rules, the only ones that truly count are the ones that your core and must-have customers have. If you know their rules and play by them, your customers will be fiercely loyal to you and your business will thrive. Unfortunately, customers' rules aren't posted as clearly as the No Shirt, No

Shoes, No Service sign in diners. To paraphrase your favorite television judge, ignorance of the rules is no excuse. It's up to you to find out what they are. **Not knowing—or not paying attention to the rules—is the fastest way to get bumped from your must-have customer's short list of companies to do business with.**

The only way to find out what your core and must-have customers' rules are is to ask them. I'll get into the specifics of how that's done below, but first I want to give you an example of what can happen if you don't spend the time to get to know your core and must-have customers' rules. Actually in this case, it's not just a single company that doesn't understand the rules, but an entire industry.

A Cautionary Tale . . .

Back in the early 1990s, when e-commerce was just getting off the ground, the major department stores began to notice that sales were declining and they were losing market share to online retailers. They hired some consultants who told them that the way to turn their business around was to focus on customer service. The retailers brought in a bunch of customer service experts, but sales continued to slide. So they hired some new consultants, who told them that their prices were too high. The stores started stocking cheaper brands, ran a lot of promotions, and focused their advertising on low prices. But market share kept slipping, and it's been heading south ever since.

Why? Years ago, department stores' core customers were older and more affluent and so were their must-have customers. But today, department stores' merchandising and advertising focuses on much less affluent customers—and that's exactly who they are attracting. What's wrong with that? After all, these new customers come into the department stores ready to spend money, right? Well, yes, but they're attracted mostly by low-price sale items. They can't afford most of the other, more expensive merchandise—the stuff that generates the profits.

For the past five years, my company has conducted the National Shopping Behavior Study for one of our clients. This annual study, done right after Christmas, tracks changes in the shopping behavior of retail consumers. Looking at the results over time, we found that the percentage of consumers who name department stores as the place where they spend the most declined from 15 percent in 2000 to 11 percent in 2004. That was no big surprise—everyone already knew that department stores were in trouble. But we went the extra step and actually found out *why* department store shoppers were shifting their business to specialty stores, catalogs, and the Internet (vital information that didn't seem to interest those consultants I mentioned earlier).

The answer? Department stores' core customers—shoppers with incomes over $75,000 per year—are looking for selection. But their definition of *selection* went beyond "having a huge inventory." To affluent shoppers, selection means "the things I want, in the colors I like, and in a size that fits me." And they're willing to pay a premium to get it. While it's always nice to find a helpful salesperson, and nobody will ever complain about getting a good deal, selection is what attracts affluent customers and gets them to open their wallets.

If you want proof, look no further than Nordstrom,

which has built a reputation for offering a superior selection of merchandise and uncompromising customer service. Management has a crystal-clear view of their core and must-have customers, stocks the merchandise that customers say they want and actually buy, has stayed far away from the price promotion arena, and is outperforming every other department store chain. Many smaller, specialty stores have imitated Nordstrom's model very successfully. Customers routinely single out Ann Taylor, Gap, Talbots, Chico's, and Victoria's Secret for their great selection.

Every once in a while I'll meet a retail industry consultant, one of those people who bills himself as the ultimate maven, who claims to know so much about consumers and their behavior that he doesn't actually need to do any research. People like this have made a career out of convincing their clients, and anyone else who'll listen, that "customers don't really know what they want"—in other words, they don't have any rules. A piece of advice: If anyone tells you that, politely end the conversation and get away as quickly as possible. **The truth is that *all* customers have rules and they know *exactly* what they want.**

If you want to find out what they are, all you have to do is ask. Chances are, they'll give you a very clear, specific, and coherent answer.

Along the same lines, be very careful of any salesperson who claims that "I talked them out of what they really wanted." Yes, it's possible for a customer to be pressured into something. Even so, after the salesperson is gone and the customer is left alone to reconsider his or her decision, what seemed like a short-term victory will probably turn into a long-term loss. But again, *selection* isn't about having a lot, it's about having what your core and must-have customers want. To summarize, if your products or services or policies conflict with customers' rules, they'll vote with their feet and buy from your competition.

Ask, Ask, Ask . . .

Knowing your customers' rules—what's critical to them and exactly what you have to do to meet their needs—is the key to attracting and keeping loyal customers. And, as I mentioned above, if you don't already know the rules, your core and must-have customers will be glad to tell them to you. But they won't say anything unless you ask them. You'd think that would be simple enough, but it's amazing how many otherwise intelligent managers never bother to ask their core customers why they stick around, their must-have customers what keeps them from being actual customers, and their former customers why they left. Instead, they rely on "mother-in-law" research, randomly asking friends or relatives why they shop or eat or buy where they do. This information is absolutely useless. Asking employees' opinions is worse than useless, since they generally give the answers they think their managers want to hear instead of the answers management really needs to hear.

Another reason not to ask employees to tell you what customers want is that their information is often old or flawed. People who've been with a company ten, fifteen, or twenty years often assume that what was true when they first started in the business still is. And sometimes an employee's interpretation of customers' needs is based on an experience with a few particularly vocal customers who may or may not be representative of the whole core or must-have customer base.

Of those companies that actually do customer research, many stick only with top-of-mind questions, such as, Are our customers satisfied? But remember, satisfaction is nothing more than "not dissatisfied enough to make a change right now." It's not a measure of loyalty and it's not a guarantee that your customers will ever buy from you again. A far better approach is to ask questions that are designed around the theme of, **Why are our satisfied customers buying from our competition and what do we have to do to make them stop?** Focusing on these questions will give you very specific, actionable data on whether your core and must-have customers are loyal and what you need to do to make them loyal if they're not, what you're doing wrong that sent previously satisfied customers to your competition, and what you need to change in order to keep that from happening again.

———

The following questions are designed to be used in a blind survey (meaning that the participants don't know which company is asking the questions) with three groups of customers: core, must-have, and former must-haves or cores. Again, asking any other customers but these will skew your data and produce inaccurate results.

- Where do you spend the most for (the name of the product or service)? Why?
  - Second most? Why?
  - Third most? Why
- Who is the best supplier of (the name of the product or service)? Why? If you could buy (the name of the product or service) only from one supplier, who would you buy from? Why?
- What do you really love about your current supplier?
- What annoys you about your current supplier?
- What would you require of a new supplier to switch your business?

- If you could create a perfect supplier, how would it be different from your current supplier?
  - How would it be different from the other suppliers in the market?

You will, of course, have to adapt these questions to your specific business situation. If you're running a retail company, for example, you'll want to know the demographics of your customers and the lifestyle choices and values that drive them to purchase. If you're running a manufacturing company, you'll need to know whether your must-have customers put price or quality first.

Regardless of the kind of business you're in, keep in mind that good research *always* uses questions that are precisely framed. Only the right questions asked the right way will get your core customers to tell you what you're doing right and what you're not. It will also tell you exactly why your core customers are buying from you and why your must-haves with similar characteristics aren't.

... And Ask Some More

Asking questions is actually a two-part process. The second part—listening to the answers—may be even more important then the first. And by "listening to the answers," I mean truly listening. No second-guessing, no mind reading. If your customers tell you something you don't understand, ask a few follow-ups to make sure you've got it. If you aren't sure what you'd need to do to meet their needs, ask them. Too many companies fall into the trap of thinking they know what customers want. The results can be devastating.

In the late 1990s, McDonald's, the world's largest restaurant chain, was losing volume and market share, and they wanted to know why. So they commissioned some research and found that customers thought McDonald's food quality had deteriorated. One of the Company's major competitors, Burger King, was still offering "Have It Your Way." You remember the jingle—"Hold the pickles, hold the lettuce—special orders don't upset us"—that launched the advertising campaign in 1974? Well, more than thirty years later,

Burger King is still offering customers the opportunity to have food prepared their way. In response to both of these factors, McDonald's food engineers created the Made for You system, which was designed to make it possible for customers to get their meals made to order. Individual items were prepared in advance and kept in warming trays. When an order came in for a Big Mac with extra pickles and no onion, it could be assembled easily.

McDonald's and its franchisees spent hundreds of millions of dollars installing all of the new specially designed equipment and retraining their staff. The outcome was almost perfect. Restaurants were now able to deliver food to their customers that was hotter, fresher, and just the way the customer wanted it. The only problem was that now it took about twice as long to get an order filled as before.

McDonald's Made for You program was the product of two significant mistakes. First, as we talked about in the previous chapter, the company responded to what a competitor—Burger King—was doing instead of solidifying its own sweet spot in the market.

Second and most important, McDonald's management didn't have a clear understanding of what its customers' rules were. They assumed that the "deteriorating quality" problem could be solved by making the food fresh, even if it took a little longer. But what customers really wanted was fast service with acceptable-tasting food. In their minds, there wasn't much difference between food they didn't like that's been sitting around for a while and food they didn't like that was freshly prepared. What they ended up with was the same old food, delivered slowly. Not surprisingly, McDonald's continued to lose volume and share, and in January 2003, the company posted its first ever quarterly loss.

Fortunately, it's never too late to start asking the right questions and listening to the answers. Consider what happened to McDonald's after they got rid of the Made for You campaign—and then-CEO Jack Greenberg. The new CEO, Jim Cantalupo, took a closer look at customer preferences and found, as Greenberg did, that food quality was the barrier keeping McDonald's must-have customers away. But instead of thinking that food quality issues could be solved by serving fresher versions of the same food, Cantalupo took some steps to give must-have customers what they really needed and expected. Chicken parts were replaced by "real" chicken strips. Cheap lettuce was replaced by a mix of better greens. The cheapest salad dressing money could buy was replaced with Paul Newman's "Newman's Own" dressings. New items, such as premium salads, McGriddle's breakfast sandwiches, and yogurt parfaits were added to the menus. McDonald's was now meeting its must-have customers' rules by giving them better-tasting, better-quality food delivered quickly. As a result, McDonald's is showing same-store growth and dramatically improved financial results.

Another example of a company that almost went off half-cocked is Whirlpool, which nearly became the victim of some very bad advice. In 1991, Boston Consulting, one of the most respected consulting firms in the country, suggested that Whirlpool begin deemphasizing its small dealer network. These small dealers were being served by eight hundred traveling salespeople who met in person with each of their customers three or four times a year. The salespeople would take Charlie the dealer to lunch, talk about fishing and the family, and then move on to the next little town. The ratio of cost to sales was astronomical, but the company was reluctant to get rid of the sales force because they thought that there was a lot of value in the salesman-dealer relationships.

According to Boston Consulting, Home Depot, Circuit City, Best Buy, and other big chains were going to put the little guys out of business and Whirlpool should get out immediately. They suggested setting up a call center so that any of the small dealers who managed to survive could call in if they needed something. Since I'd done some work for Whirlpool on another project, they asked me to set up the call center.

Before starting the project, I suggested that we spend some time getting to know the customers' rules. I put together a survey of about four hundred dealers—a good-size cross-section of their entire network—with the goal of understanding how they felt about the service they were currently receiving, what Whirlpool was currently doing for them that they didn't consider valuable, and what kinds of services the dealers felt they really wanted. The first thing that came out of the research was that the dealers felt they had no relationship with Whirlpool's sales force at all and that they weren't getting serviced at all. Most said that almost all the communication they had with Whirlpool salespeople was through voice mail. Getting taken out to lunch a few times a year didn't make a bit of difference to them.

After brainstorming about ways to improve service to the dealers, I suggested to Whirlpool that they create a telesales organization to replace the salespeople. This organization would be the exact opposite of the passive, call-receiving center that Boston Consulting had suggested. By hiring people with the talent to contact the dealers and sell them what they needed by phone, Whirlpool could actually increase the frequency of contact, improve its relationships with the dealers, provide better service, and reduce costs.

We designed a call center in Knoxville, Tennessee, based on the specific systems and processes that would meet the dealers' rules. Talented people for every position in the facility were carefully chosen using sophisticated selection tools. For seven consecutive years, the telesales organization has generated over a 15 percent sales increase each year. This program was so successful that Whirlpool expanded it to several other countries, where it's producing comparable results.

Loyalty and Your Sweet Spot: You Don't Have to Play by Everyone's Rules

There's a good chance that after asking the must-know questions I outlined above you'll discover that you aren't satisfying some of your core and must-have customers' needs, and that some of your supposedly satisfied core and must-have customers really aren't, and are just biding their time before moving on. There's also a good chance that those discoveries will trigger a knee-jerk desire to make a lot of changes in order to keep from losing customers. Don't—or at least not yet. It's critical as you evaluate the results of your research to stay focused on the sweet spot you identified in Chapter 3. Making some changes will help you strengthen and perhaps expand your sweet spot. Others will weaken it.

Think about Wal-Mart, the biggest retailer in the

world. As big as they are, they don't—and don't want to—play by every possible customer's rules. Instead, they play only by the rules of the customers who help the company maintain its sweet spot, customers who are looking for basic merchandise and clothing at the lowest price. Wal-Mart knows that millions of people drive right by a Wal-Mart on the way to Kohl's, Toys R Us, Walgreens, Target, Best Buy, and dozens of other retailers. Those customers have rules—better selection, more fashionable merchandise, better quality—that Wal-Mart doesn't want to play by.

Once you've matched up your must-have customers' rules to your sweet spot, the next step is to do whatever is necessary to make as many of them as you can become loyal. How, exactly, you do that relates back to the definition of customers' rules that I gave at the beginning of this chapter: ". . . the policies, beliefs, desires, expectations, and needs that together support their buying decisions." The two key words here are "needs" and "expectations."

Indulge me for a minute and visualize something. Your relationship with your customers is like a high school dance. You're on one side of the gym and your must-have customer is on the other. You've smiled at each other from across the room and you think it might be nice to dance together. But in order to do so, you'll have to go all the way across the dance floor and make contact. The problem is that it's a long walk, and there are all sorts of other people just as cute as you are who'd like to dance with your customer, too.

That wide expanse of dance floor between you and your customer is the difference between your customers' needs and expectations and what you're doing to satisfy them. The bigger that space, the more likely it is that your customers will go home with someone else. The smaller the space, the sooner you'll be able to start dancing with each other and the longer you'll stay together. The more you know what your customers need and expect and the better you satisfy them, the more loyal they'll be.

Of course, on your way across the dance floor, you need to keep an eye out for other opportunities. Customers sometimes change their rules and someone you never thought you'd have anything to do with can suddenly become irresistible.

This is exactly what happened in 2001 in the airline business. Southwest Airlines was the pioneer in low-cost, no-frills air travel and had built its business by appealing to leisure customers who care more about a cheap airfare than amenities that jack up the price of the ticket. To meet its customers' rules, Southwest flies out of secondary, less costly airports, serves peanuts for meals, and has no assigned seating. But after 9/11, the economy went into a bit of a slump, budgets were cut, and business travelers could no longer afford expensive tickets. As a result, a lot of business travelers changed their rules from "we need to get there now so we don't care what it costs" to "we want cheaper prices for eleventh-hour tickets or trips without a Saturday night stay."

United, American, and USAir didn't see this change in rules and they kept charging their core customers the same old exorbitant prices. Southwest, though, didn't miss a beat and went dancing away with the big carriers' former core customers.

Not All Loyalties Are Created Equal

One of the hallmarks of loyal customers is that they buy from you over and over. But while making purchases is certainly a good thing, it's important to keep in mind that loyalty actually involves two separate components: attitude and behavior. *Attitude,* as you might expect, is the collection of thoughts, beliefs, and emotions that a consumer has about your particular product, service, or brand. *Behavior* is following through on those attitudes and making a purchase. Truly loyal customers exhibit the right attitude *and* the right behavior. Having one without the other may produce some short-term gains, but they won't last. I will give you a couple of examples.

Loyal Behavior Without Loyal Attitude

This scenario usually happens in monopoly situations. Before 1984, if you wanted to make a long-distance phone call in the United States, you probably had a choice between AT&T, AT&T, and AT&T. Consumers' behavior was loyal, but they weren't happy about it. And the minute the Department of Justice split Ma Bell into the seven Baby Bells, a lot of those seemingly loyal customers jumped ship.

Similarly, millions of people were loyal to Microsoft's Internet Explorer—not because they loved it, but because it was nearly impossible to buy a PC without one. After Microsoft got slapped by the Justice Department, a lot of people dumped IE.

Loyal Attitude Without Loyal Behavior

For many years I was a Lexus man. I'd owned a 300 ES sedan and a 450 SUV. After a problem with the SUV's suspension was corrected, I was totally satisfied with its performance. During the Colorado winters, I was always confident that it would get me safely between the Denver International Airport and my home in the mountains, often in conditions that would have sidelined other vehicles in its class. When the odometer on the 450 rolled over the 115,000 mile mark, I decided it was time to buy a new SUV.

My initial thought was to buy the Lexus 470, the newer model of the 450. So I made my first—and what I thought would be my only—shopping trip: to the Lexus dealer. The 470 was beautiful and could be customized with all sorts of great techno toys. The brochure was world-class and emphasized the prestige and status of owning a Lexus. My ego loved it.

Naturally, the dealer had ordered every car fully loaded with every conceivable gadget, including a $2,000 navigation system that could accurately direct me down Interstate 70 to the airport. Given that I have completely memorized that route, even including the cellular phone dead spots, a high-priced navigation system was a complete waste of money. For a few minutes I rationalized the $71,000 sticker price and was ready to pick my color and do my part to keep Lexus's retention rate high. But for some reason I decided to hold off for a few days.

Since I was very satisfied with the Lexus brand, it had never occurred to me to look anywhere else. But several friends suggested that I shop around. After doing a little research, I discovered that I would be paying a $15,000 premium for the Lexus status badge. That plus the memory of the earlier suspension problem convinced me that it was time to make my search more objective and less ego-driven.

Although I'm still a Lexus fan, I'm now the owner of a Volvo XC90. It's not as luxurious as the Lexus 470, but it has better pickup, and it handles the twists and turns like my eighteen-year-old Nissan 300XZ (which I still love driving through those curvy, mountain roads). My satisfaction with Lexus cost the company a sale.

Loyalty: It's a Continuum, Not a Destination

One of the most important things to remember about loyalty is that it's something that you can never truly achieve. Customers' rules are constantly changing. Usually the changes are a lot more subtle than the ones that affected the airlines after 9/11. But big or small, if you don't keep up with the new rules, the results can be the same: bankruptcy. So once you've determined your customers' current requirements and taken steps to meet them, it's critical to do ongoing research to make sure that you're always on target. The information you receive can help you improve the products or services you sell, which will greatly enhance your chances of creating lasting customer loyalty.

One of the best examples of a company that does regular, in-depth research is Coach, a leader in fashion accessories such as handbags, belts, gloves, and scarves. Coach had sales of $1.32 billion in fiscal 2004—a 39 percent increase over the previous year—and net income was up 78.5 percent. Between 2002 and 2005, the value of one share of Coach stock increased in value by a factor of six.

Coach spends $2 million a year on consumer surveys. A year before it introduces products, it surveys hundreds of core customers on the aspects of new designs, such as strap length and styling and ranks them against existing merchandise. Six months before a new collection is rolled out, products are tested in a cross section of stores around the country.

According to the company's Web site, "Perhaps the

most important element of the Coach competitive proposition is our loyal and involved customer. Coach consumers had a specific emotional connection with the brand. Our database allows us to reach millions of active Coach users, and every day we work to reinforce this emotional connection through our Internet, advertising, and direct marketing communications. As a result of these ongoing efforts, approximately nine out of ten Coach consumers express a positive intent to repurchase." Judging from the numbers above, it's pretty clear that these efforts have been worthwhile.

Once a year, one of my industrial clients asks its customers to rate the company and how it compares to direct competitors. The information we collect is used to improve the company's processes, and changes are continuously tracked to make sure that the customers' expectations are always being met or exceeded. Loyal customers are the natural byproduct of this kind of process, and they're directly responsible for the company's better-than-the-industry-average performance. In each of the past fourteen years, the company has had a compound annual increase in sales of 20 percent.

Loyalty Programs:
The Good, the Bad, and Mostly the Ugly

One of the best—and worst—ways to attract and keep loyal customers is by using a loyalty program. The world is full of them. You can join one at grocery stores, drugstores, airlines, car rental places, video stores, hotels, and dozens of others. U.S. businesses spend over $1 billion every year on their loyalty programs and about 75 percent of U.S. consumers say they belong to at least one.

That 75 percent figure is great if the goal of a loyalty program is to get people to sign up for a card. But if the goal is to create loyal customers who buy your product or service again and again and again, the insane proliferation of cards isn't worth much. A great loyalty program with plentiful points is no substitute for selling the wrong product, the wrong service, or the wrong price. It simply doesn't work.

The true reason loyalty programs exist is so that companies can track members' shopping patterns and make sure they're getting what they want. Properly run, loyalty programs can become a revenue source and play a vital role in the success of a company. It costs a lot less to retain a customer than to bring in a new one, and loyalty programs can help increase retention rates while lowering the cost even further. But badly run—which most are—they're actually a drain on the company, costing a lot to administer and adding very little value to the customer.

I travel a lot for business, and everywhere I go I rent a car. I'm a Hertz Gold Club member because of the convenience and speed of service. The shuttle bus picks me up at the airport terminal and drops me off at my car. A printed rental agreement is inside, and many times the trunk is open and the motor running. Convenience and fast service are very important to me, so I'm loyal to Hertz, but it's *despite* their program, not because of it. Somewhere in their computers, Hertz has a complete record of my rental patterns, including the number of days I usually rent, cities where I rent, whether I get the optional insurance, whether I bring the car back with a full tank, whether I've ever used any of their coupons, and a lot more. But they choose to ignore all that, and a few times a year send me the same package of offers that every Gold Club member gets. Why offer me thirty dollars off a weekly rental or a free day on a three-day rental if I've never rented a car for more than two days? Why bother to mail out certificates for one-class upgrades if they can't be guaranteed in advance? Hertz is wasting a huge amount of money and producing zero results from me.

Hertz is outdone in senseless loyalty program rules only by United Airlines, which I fly frequently—again, despite their program. As a 1K member who flies over 100,000 miles per year, I periodically receive coupons for a free round-trip ticket. These are usable only on designated seats (W, S, T, or whatever letter is available at the time) and not upgradeable to first class. Any other ticket could be upgraded for fifty dollars per five hundred miles. Why not make me a happier customer by letting me buy upgrades on a free ticket?

Many companies use loyalty programs as a way to get around fundamental problems they don't know how to fix. They haven't figured out who their must-have customers are and they haven't identified their sweet

ROBERT GORDMAN

spot; they don't know how to differentiate their offerings from their competition's and make what they're selling more desirable to their must-have customers.

Survey after survey shows that most consumers rate other factors, such as selection, quality, service, convenience, and the ability to return merchandise far higher than the existence of a reward program. And plenty of very successful companies have done quite well without a program. Costco, Wal-Mart, Target, Whole Foods, and others execute great strategies, understand and play by their customers' rules, and don't resort to gimmicks to bring people through the doors.

Okay, now that you've seen a few examples of loyalty programs that don't work, let me tell you about two that do. First, Harrah's Entertainment. A few months ago I spoke with Harrah's senior vice president of relationship marketing, David Norton, who gave me some wonderful insights into their program.

First, a little history. Until 1976, Nevada was the only state that allowed casino gaming. Since then, all but two states, Utah and Hawaii, have legalized some form of commercial gambling. Across the country there are hundreds of casinos in operation and thousands of state lottery games, horse and dog tracks, jai alai arenas, bingo halls, keno games, and gaming machines such as slots, video poker, and video roulette.

Harrah's had been using customer rewards cards. But those programs generally failed to bring in any new revenue and actually cost the company money. What the company did have, though, was a lot of data. Management started analyzing the mass of customer information, and in the process discovered Harrah's core customer. They were the low rollers, the 30 percent of customers who spent between $100 and $499 a trip but produced a startling 80 percent of the company's revenue and close to 100 percent of the profits. This target group became Harrah's must-have customers.

In 1997, Harrah's started its Total Gold frequent-gambler card, which it has since renamed the Total Rewards program. In the beginning, the program wasn't particularly attractive to the low rollers, who weren't earning freebies fast enough to make a difference. Under the current program, cardholders can earn different types of points that qualify them for anything from free rooms to DVD players—whatever the customer wants, as opposed to some low-level reward determined by the company. Cardholders who reach certain levels of spending become eligible for Platinum or Diamond memberships, each of which offers its own perks, such as special lounges, free limo service, and more.

To say that the Total Rewards program is a success would be an incredible understatement. Today, Harrah's tracks over 75 percent of its revenue—up from less than 50 percent just a few years ago. In addition, customers are spending more of their total gaming budget at Harrah's—43 percent in 2002, up from 36 percent in 1997. The company also enjoys a 95 percent occupancy rate, far higher than the industry average of about 60 percent and a Las Vegas average of 80 percent. They attribute the high occupancy rate to data gathered from Total Rewards members, which allows the company to tailor its promotions to highly targeted groups of customers. Using data collected from its customers, Harrah's even redesigned its casino floors to increase the number of low-denomination slots and video poker machines. The result? A 12 percent increase in slot revenues. Among its top hotel, casino, and resort competitors, Harrah's is ranked number one in profits as a percent of revenue, as a percent of assets, and as a percent of shareholder equity. It is also number one in annual earnings-per-share growth from 1991 through 2002 and in total return to investors in 2001.

Now, I know that Harrah's has the kind of financial resources to do almost any kind of customer research it wants to. But almost any company, regardless of size, could create a similar program. You don't have to hire a bunch of PhDs in math from MIT or Harvard MBAs. Simply knowing who your must-have customers are, continually asking them to tell you how to improve, and then taking their advice will produce dramatic results. And, as David Norton told me, these things (ongoing research and doing what's necessary to create loyal customers) have a way of snowballing. Once you've shown your customers that you care enough to ask for their opinion and to follow through on it, they'll be back—with a few of their friends. And that's the kind of results that no loyalty program can produce by itself.

Loblaw, Canada's largest food distributor, has one of the most interesting loyalty programs that I've seen. Rather than start a grocery-based program—where cardholders get special prices on selected items—Loblaw partnered with a huge Canadian bank and created President's Choice Financial, a service for customers who want to open up checking accounts, get low-interest mortgages, and apply for a President's Choice MasterCard. Every time a cardholder uses his card or makes a mortgage payment or a savings deposit, he earns points that are redeemable for groceries, travel, and so on.

A Final Thought on Loyalty Programs

When you give a gift, open your hand all the way. I can't imagine anything worse than giving your best, most important, and most profitable customers a half-hearted gift. If you can't afford the gift, don't do anything. Keep your asset protection and policy geeks away from your program. While they're watching the pennies, your bottom line will bleed dollars. Remember these are your best customers, the ones that keep your company alive and represent your future.

Conclusion

At the very beginning of this chapter I said there's a big difference between satisfied customers and loyal customers: **Satisfaction is temporary. Loyalty can be forever.** The operative words are "can be." Keeping a loyal customer loyal is a never-ending effort. It has to become part of the infrastructure of your company, as much a reflex action as turning on the light switches in your office.

For many years I kept my family's cash and investment accounts with one brokerage firm. In the spring of 2003, I received a nice letter from the firm announcing their new "special services" program for larger customers. The letter was followed a week later by a call from my new special services adviser. He introduced me to the benefits of this new program, let me know that he and his team were available seven days a week to me, and even offered a free portfolio review.

Needless to say, I was pleased and impressed. No question about it, the firm's special program was making me feel special.

Over the next year or so, my special services adviser checked in once in a while. But after that, I stopped hearing from him. I'm not sure whether I lost my status as a "special customer," the company dropped the program, or my adviser left the company. Whatever the reason, I stopped feeling special, and I'm no longer loyal.

At this point, you know exactly who your core and must-have customers are and what values are most important to them. You know where your core and must-have customers have positioned you in the marketplace, and you know who your real competitors are and how you stack up against them. You've created a defensible sweet spot, and you're turning your satisfied customers into loyal ones.

If you've done all that, I can guarantee that your company is better off than when you started this book, and you're perfectly positioned for long-term, sustainable growth. But before you go out and buy something really expensive on credit, we've got a little more work to do. And the first item on the agenda is to pinpoint exactly what's critical for your business to succeed.

STEP 5

Critical Success Factors: Do You Know What You Don't Know?

Take a look at your PDA. If yours is like mine, it's filled with all sorts of to-do items and lists: meetings, phone calls to return, projects to complete, sales goals to achieve, job vacancies to fill, and so on. There is one item I'll bet you *don't* have in your PDA or anywhere else. It's a *specific, detailed list of the three items that are critical to your company's success.* And you're definitely not alone.

As managers, we're so inundated with reports and information, and there are so many details involved in running the business on a day-to-day basis, that it's easy to lose track of what we really need to do to keep the business alive. I'm not just talking about what's important here, I'm talking about what's *critical*. The two words "important" and "critical" may sound very similar, but the distinction is one that can make or break your company.

Let me give you a classic example. Back in the early 1960s, imported cars accounted for less than 1 percent of the total U.S. market. But starting in about 1970, imports, mainly from Japan, started pouring in. These cars were better made, more fuel efficient, and less expensive than American cars. Top execs at the Big Three thought that while quality and fuel efficiency were important to American car buyers, flashy new designs and powerful engines were critical. As it turns out, they had it exactly backwards. Style and power were important, but what Americans *really* wanted—what was a critical factor in their car-buying decisions—were quality, reliability, and fuel efficiency. Just take a look at one of the best-selling cars in history, the Toyota Corolla: not a car that many people would call "stylish."

By 1974, the Big Three's miscalculation of their

critical success factors had enabled imports to increase their share of the U.S. market to almost 20 percent. That percentage rose steadily until American automakers finally got the message and started producing better-made, more fuel-efficient cars. Even today, over 30 percent of cars sold in the United States are foreign imports.

Ask the Right Questions

Why do so many companies have trouble distinguishing between the critical and the merely important? Simply put, they ask the wrong questions. Most managers, for example, ask, What are our priorities? or, What are we going to do to make the next quarter? Questions like those typically generate twenty or thirty answers and an avalanche of data that can crush your business. With so much information to filter through, companies then try to prioritize. I've seen a lot of corporate priority lists, and I can tell you that most of the items are either impractical or deal only with achieving short-term goals. In other words, they don't have much to do with the long-term health of the organization.

As a result, companies slip into crisis management mode, which helps them solve their immediate problems. Don't get me wrong: Crisis management can be a lot of fun. I've done it more than once in companies that I've run and with clients. Crisis management gets the adrenaline pumping, gets people motivated to work harder, and a lot of exciting changes can happen very quickly.

All that's fine for a while, but over the long haul, a short-term, crisis-oriented mentality is dangerous. **You may be able to temporarily reduce expenses, but you'll never deal with the underlying problems that caused the crisis in the first place.** Almost invariably, the problem will come up again, and you'll have to go into crisis mode again. At some point, you'll no longer be able to cut costs without also cutting quality, productivity, and/or customer service.

Success isn't a random occurrence or something that just naturally happens. Very often companies are successful, but don't know why or how that success happened. Growing a company is a process of continually repeating success. It's critical for companies to have a process to create sustained profitable growth. Management needs to know what creates success as well as failure. If you're not sure what created the success, how can you repeat it? If you don't know what caused a failure, how can you avoid it?

The solution? Ask better questions. Instead of, What are our priorities? or, How are we going to get through this crisis? the real question is, What is critical to our success? What you're looking for here is a maximum of two or three concrete, long-term initiatives that will focus your entire organization on a process of continuous improvement.

You won't be able to answer that all-important question right now. But over the next few pages, I'll show you exactly how.

Creating Success with a Strategic Plan

The "specific, detailed, process for creating success" that I mentioned at the beginning of this chapter is also called a *strategic plan.* And that's essentially a map that plots out the path your company will take from where it is now to where it realistically can be. Your strategic plan will be based on all the information you've gathered in Chapters 1 through 4 of this book. Properly constructed, it will identify your company's critical success factors and articulate the precise steps you need to take to achieve and sustain that success. A successful strategic plan includes *all* of the following components:

- Focus on *what's* right instead of *who's* right.
- Ask the right people.
- Dig deeper into the data you already have.
- Don't build consensus.
- Know what you don't know.

Let's take a look at each one of these factors in detail.

Focus on *What's* Right Instead of *Who's* Right

I'm sure at this point in your career you've had the pleasure of going through one or more strategic planning sessions. You know, the kind of meeting where the management team goes off-site for a few days, often to a nice, sunny resort, ostensibly to discuss the business. Actually, "discuss" is the wrong word—what usually happens is that strategic planning sessions turn into opportunities for the CEO or some other very vocal executives to repeat their points of view so that the rest of the management team can go back to the office and implement them.

There's no doubt that ego and self-confidence can drive people to be successful. But an overactive ego or an overdeveloped need to be right all the time, often makes executives and managers feel that they have to continually remind everyone in the organization who's in charge. They spend their time giving orders and making demands instead of asking questions and listening. When your focus is on *who's* right, you'll spend a disproportionate amount of time heatedly arguing about ideas that have no positive influence on your business. Egos reign, no one wants to lose face by backing down, and facts only confuse the discussion. Eventually, the guy with the corner office (or the loudest voice) wins.

In *Good to Great,* Jim Collins writes about five

types of leaders: Level 1 is a highly capable individual, Level 2 is a contributing team member, Level 3 is the competent manager, Level 4 is an effective leader, and Level 5 is the executive who builds enduring greatness through a remarkable blend of personal humility and an incurable drive to make a great company. Level 5 leaders are far more interested in *doing* the right thing than in *being* right, and they achieve great things without letting their egos get in the way. Overall, they're the kind of leaders who agree completely with one of Abraham Lincoln's great quotes: "There is no limit to what you can accomplish as long as you don't care who gets the credit."

Collins found that companies run by Level 5 leaders were far more successful than those run by egocentric leaders. In fact, two-thirds of the mediocre or failing companies he analyzed were run by flashy, celebrity leaders. Focusing on what's right, and running the business on facts and not opinions, is the only way to ensure success. Life is easier for everyone, there's less pressure, and everyone has a better understanding of what they need to do to make the business flourish.

Level 5 leaders are so committed to their company's success that they typically spend a lot of time and energy preparing a successor, someone who will, hopefully, have a similar approach, and who will keep on improving the company into the future. That's exactly what Jack Welch, the former chairman and CEO of General Electric, did. Nine years before his anticipated retirement, Welch said, "From now on, choosing my successor is the most important decision I will make. It occupies a considerable amount of thought almost every day." Jack Welch's process to identify people with the potential to lead the company and then provide those individuals a broad range of operating experiences to prepare them to be CEO is legendary. When Jeff Immelt stepped in to replace Jack Welch, he was knowledgeable about all facets of the company he was to lead.

If every individual were as carefully selected and thoroughly groomed as Immelt, there would be no need for this book. Clearly, not many people in management today are as carefully and thoroughly real-world educated for their positions as they could be. Instead, companies are often run by a series of big-name, big-ego people who are more interested in leaving a legacy than in creating success. Then it's off to a new company in a new industry, without the opportunity to spend significant transition time learning the fine points of the new position from a highly successful incumbent. It's a hard cycle to break.

Ask the Right People

In large organizations, strategic planning sessions usually include managers from just about every department: HR, IT, marketing, sales, accounting, and the rest. They're a great opportunity for people who've never met to get to know and establish relationships with one another. Unfortunately, there's one rather conspicuous absence, a very important contingent that almost never gets invited to these functions: the company's core and must-have customers.

I once spent four days with one of my clients at an off-site strategic planning session. The facilitator they'd hired was a respected academic whose title was professor of strategic planning at some big university. We spent the first two days going through the standard SWOT (strengths, weaknesses, opportunities, threats) exercises. Then we got down to consensus building. The professor went around the room, gathering points of view from each individual, and wrote them all—at least twenty—on a flip chart. He then consolidated similar items and had the group vote on the four or five most important ones. What a disaster.

To start with, several of the so-called priorities reflected only a slim majority of the group. Worse than that, though, not a single one of those priorities took into account the perspectives of the client's core and must-have customers.

There's no real way to put this next sentence gently: Trying to decide in the boardroom what's critical to a company, without substantial input from core and must-have customers, is just plain dangerous. A strategic plan that is internally generated is neither strategic, nor a plan. It's nothing but a list of priorities that have a good chance of being completely irrelevant to consumers. A plan that isn't customer driven has nothing to do with reality and will almost never get implemented. In the unlikely event that it does, there's a good chance that it'll do more harm than good.

In 2001, Kmart realized that Home Depot's garden center was steadily taking market share from Kmart's garden center. So Kmart had a meeting with their management consultants (not my company), to whom they were paying a significant monthly retainer. The consultants said that since Home Depot was running a lot of television ads for its garden center, Kmart should do the same. Television advertising, they said, was a critical success factor. Were Home Depot's ads actually working? Neither Kmart nor its consultants bothered to ask any consumers.

One senior Kmart exec wasn't completely satisfied with what he was hearing, and asked me to take a look at the company's garden center business. The first thing I did was start talking to Home Depot and Kmart customers. As it turned out, advertising was the least of Kmart's problem. The real issue was that only a very small percentage of Kmart's core customers were even aware that Kmart had a garden center. Home Depot's garden center was right up front, where almost everyone coming into the store could see it.

Kmart's centers were an afterthought, stuck in a corner at the back of the stores—about as far away as possible from the main flow of customers. If you didn't know it was there you'd walk right by, which is exactly what most people did.

And that's only the beginning. Because of the loss of garden center market share, Kmart decided to reduce expenses by cutting garden center payroll and stocking lower-quality live plants. Instead, they put their money into stocking a line of designer gardening tools. As a result, there wasn't enough staff to care for the plants. So the few customers who actually ventured into Kmart's garden center found a poor selection of cheap, half-dead plants. The fact that they could buy a Martha Stewart garden hose was lost on them. Clearly, while advertising was important and may have brought more people into Kmart stores, brand-name implements were completely irrelevant. Finding the garden center and being able to buy nice, healthy plants were critical success factors.

I submitted my report to the senior executive I was working with. He showed it to Kmart's CEO, who promptly ignored it. Instead, he followed the advice of the nationally recognized consultants he trusted (even though they hadn't talked to a single Kmart customer) and launched an aggressive television campaign. The results were even worse than the previous season. Sadly, this wasn't an isolated case. Not getting customer input before making life-and-death decisions was almost a religious experience for Kmart. And, as I've mentioned before, they paid a pretty heavy price.

Recognize that Customer Data Has Its Limitations

As much as I've emphasized the importance of customers and what they say, you can't rely on them exclusively. In 2004 and 2005, we had the opportunity to work with Atlanta-based Rhodes Furniture. Rhodes was the eighth-largest furniture retailer in the country, but having some serious sales and profit problems. As part of our standard diagnostics we conducted the first consumer research ever done by the company, completed a thorough analysis of all internal data, conducted discussion groups with top management, best store managers, and best salespeople.

As I discussed in Chapter 1, Rhodes didn't know who their core customers were, which, of course, kept them from identifying their must-have customers. Recent Rhodes customers thought Rhodes was okay, but not compelling. Many used Rhodes to fill in items around the major purchases they made at other stores, and most Rhodes customers named another furniture store as the place they would go to first for their next purchase.

Rhodes management was reluctant to make any changes, and so their problems continued until July 2004 when Steve Fishman took over as CEO. Fishman quickly saw that one-third of the stores and two-thirds of the distribution facilities were highly unprofitable or seriously inefficient, and he realized that the only way the company could survive was to go through Chapter 11.

Chapter 11 helped relieve the pressure and allowed Rhodes to reestablish relationships with vendors. Utilizing the research and sales data analysis, we identified the core and must-have customers, and we assisted

Rhodes's management with the restructuring of just about every facet of the company.

Our core and must-have customers told us they weren't satisfied with the merchandise. We fixed it. They told us that the advertising didn't motivate them to shop at Rhodes. We fixed it. An analysis of the balance sheet told us that the company couldn't survive with highly unprofitable stores. We fixed that. Our must-have customers told us what was wrong with the store layouts, signage, and customer service policies. We fixed those, too. And on and on through every element of the business.

Only five months after filing Chapter 11, Rhodes was already showing improved sales and profits—but it wasn't enough. No question, all the changes we made were important, yet we'd missed the *critical* success factor. More about that in the next section.

Dig Deeper into the Data You Already Have

If you've been following the steps outlined in the previous chapters, you've got all the data you need to create a solid strategic plan. In fact, you probably have more than enough. Now you need to analyze it. I know, you already have, but humor me and do it again. But this time, dig a little deeper. Follow threads you initially thought don't go anywhere; try correlating items that seem completely unrelated. If you can, have someone who doesn't know your business take a look and see what interesting trends he or she can come up with. Doing this kind of creative data mining proved to be the turning point for Rhodes.

Looking for opportunities to improve efficiencies and trim unnecessary expenses, we started looking at P&Ls on a store-by-store basis. Some, we found, were more profitable than others—nothing eye-opening there. Then we had a meeting with the CEO, who had just come back from visiting one of the company's stores in St. Louis. The store was in a run-down building in an industrial neighborhood. Fishman didn't think the company could justify keeping this store open. At first we agreed, but when we looked at the data from that store we were surprised to see that it was one of the most profitable stores in the company. We wanted to know why, so we started looking at the data all over again.

We ran the numbers in all sorts of different ways and didn't come up with much—until we started talking about the company's nine hundred salespeople. As at most furniture companies, Rhodes's salespeople were paid 100 percent on commission. If they didn't sell, they didn't eat. In addition, every salesperson had to meet a quota (in Rhodes's case, $40,000 per month) or risk being put on probation.

During the discussion I asked one of the VPs how many hours a week each salesperson worked. He said they were all full-time, but just to be sure I had one of my analysts—a truly brilliant guy—go through the payroll data.

Now, here's where the bring-in-someone-with-a-different-perspective thing comes in. My analyst, Chris Rozniecki, a twenty-five-year retail veteran, started asking a bunch of nonfurniture questions. The first thing we learned was that there was not only a huge range in hours worked, but that all the salespeople—whether they worked twenty or forty or sixty hours per week—had to hit the same $40,000-per-month target. Some were putting in sixty hours a week and barely hitting the target. Others were doubling or tripling the target in twenty hours per week.

Breaking that into sales per hour produced a fascinating insight. Some salespeople were selling over $600 worth of furniture per hour, while others were selling as little as $228. When we reported this to Rhodes management, their initial reaction was, "So what?" So we explained why this was such an important piece of information. At one of the stores that was about to be closed, there were two salespeople who were selling at the $228-per-hour rate. Replacing those two people with $600-per-hour salespeople would have generated $372 per hour more in sales. In just the previous twelve months, those poor sellers—who, fortunately, were working only twenty hours per week—had cost the company more than $750,000, easily the difference between closing a store and keeping it open. Had they put in forty hours a week, the annual difference would have been $1.5 million!

The moral of the story is that by taking a fresh look at data Rhodes already had, and analyzing it using different criteria than had ever been considered before, we identified the single biggest critical success factor: salespeople must be able to sell. Of course, improving the look of their stores, better targeting their advertising, and changing some of their archaic policies were all important. But it was the salespeople who made the critical difference between success and failure. And until the company could hire and motivate better salespeople, any other changes would be almost purely cosmetic.

Bottom line? A weak salesperson and a good prospect make a bad combination. That's a lesson that applies to every sales-driven business, regardless of what's being sold. We'll talk more about finding and retaining "must-have employees" in the next chapter.

Don't Build Consensus

Whenever you hear the word "consensus," open your eyes wide and be very, very careful. Consensus building is a process that's designed to avoid internal disagreements. Ultimately, it's all about compromise. Decisions made by consensus have little or nothing to do with what customers require. Instead, they reflect middle ground that everyone can agree upon. Consensus building also discourages questioning and encourages rubber-stamping.

In most cases, consensus is really an excuse for inaction, or a way of deflecting blame. For instance, if used by a manager, as in "I manage by consensus," it really means, "I'm not confident in my own ability to make decisions. If I get the consensus of the group, then everyone has a share of the responsibility and I won't have to take the heat on my own if things go wrong." The result is often a series of strategies that set the company up for failure.

When a company's board of directors requires consensus from the management team, they're actually casting a clear, no-confidence vote toward the CEO. If they truly had confidence in his or her leadership, why would they require a compromise position from the management team?

Still not convinced? Well, if you believe consensus management can be productive, effective, and efficient, read the next legislative bill that comes out of Washington—a city built on consensus management.

Keep in mind that there's a big difference between consensus and getting buy-in. Effective leaders do their homework on an issue, gather relevant input, and make necessary decisions. Once that decision is made, it's communicated—along with the logic behind it— to generate acceptance and support from the rest of the team.

One final note on consensus. I'm sure the world is full of very good facilitators who clearly understand the strategic planning process and how to build a sound foundation for a strategic plan—I just haven't met very many of them. Most of the facilitators I've met do nothing more than help the management team build consensus—and they're proud of it. If you find your- self tempted to hire a facilitator, do your homework first. You want someone with a practical understanding of your industry who can lead a real strategic planning process, as opposed to a touchy-feely consensus- building session. If one promises to help you reach consensus, run the other way as fast as you can.

Know What You Don't Know

"What you don't know won't hurt you." I doubt that there's another sentence that has done more damage to American businesses. The fact is that what you don't know cannot only hurt, it can kill.

Here's one of my all-time favorite quotes: "There are known knowns. These are things we know that we know. There are known unknowns. That is to say, there are things we know we don't know. But there are also unknown unknowns. These are things we don't know we don't know."

Those pearls of wisdom came from Secretary of Defense Donald Rumsfeld, who, of course, was talking about the war on terror, but his message applies just as well to business. Every single day, unknown unknowns bring otherwise successful executives, managers, and business owners to their knees.

Now, a reasonable question at this point would be, If it's unknown, how can you know that you don't know it? It's all about preparation and ego—having the skill set to do the job, and having the common sense to get help when you need it.

At one time or another in their careers, almost everyone gets promoted. In most cases, they have the experience and the knowledge to do the new job. That's certainly not the case for everyone. Think about the top-performing salesperson who struggles as a sales manager, the gifted teacher who can't make it as a principal, the concert violinist who fails as an orchestra conductor.

All of these people have years of experience. They're smart and talented and have been very successful. Yet no matter how many hours they work, no matter how hard they try, they can't manage to get the new job done effectively. For a newly promoted manager or executive, that means not being able to build sustainable growth and profitability in his or her company, division, or business unit.

This isn't to say that people can't acquire new knowledge or develop new skills. Of course they can—but only if they recognize that they need to. Unfortunately, too many managers who find themselves in unfamiliar situations are afraid to admit that they don't know everything, or worry that they'll look stupid or incompetent or unmanagerial. Others aren't afraid—they genuinely believe that they have what it takes to do the job.

Either way, the big problem is that they don't understand the challenges they face. They focus their energy—and their employees' energy—on what they think they know instead of what's critical to the business. They create initiatives, set up measurable goals, and then pay bonuses on these feel-good goals. But without a solid understanding of the unknown unknowns, these executives are managing in the dark. They have no idea where they are, how they got there, or where the company can profitably grow. Lacking the knowledge they need to make productive decisions and give effective direction, they end up leading their companies right into the ground.

Why I Don't Perform Surgery

I've been successful in my career and have made a very good living. As a consultant I've worked in a number of industries. Of course, if I were asked to go into an operating room and perform bypass surgery, I wouldn't know what I don't know. Oh, I could probably ask some pretty good questions, like where to make the incision and how deep to cut, how to stop the bleeding, and how to put things back together. That's about as far as I could go. I could certainly take a shot at performing the surgery, but the chances of the patient surviving would be iffy at best.

Running a business may not seem nearly as precise as surgery, but in many ways it is. Could a first-time surgeon do as good a job as someone who does the same procedure three times a day? Doubtful. Would the patient recover as quickly? Probably not. Might the patient thrive for a long time to come? Hard to say.

In corporate America, it's very much the same. In many cases, a new manager's first order of business is to start cutting the fat out of his organization. It takes skill and experience to know where the fat ends and the muscle, nerves, and bones begin. When someone without relevant experience is allowed to operate, patients will die during surgery. And so will companies.

The point here is that being a success in one area is

hardly a guarantee of success in any other area. And although a podiatrist is an DPM and undoubtedly knows a lot more about anatomy than most people, you'd be a lot better off with a cardiac surgeon if you needed a heart transplant.

A Tale of GE Alumni

After Jack Welch named Jeff Immelt as his successor, three other top contenders left GE to run their own companies. The stories of Immelt, Bob Nardelli, Larry Johnston, and James McNerney underscore the importance of knowing what you don't know (or knowing what you do know) and determining the right critical success factors for a specific company.

Jeff Immelt's first big bump in the road happened on September 11, 2001, just two days after he became chairman. As Immelt explained, on September 11, "Jets with my engines hit a building I insured, [all of] which was covered by a network I owned." But according to Immelt, "GE is built to outperform." And it certainly has under Immelt's stewardship. So much so that *BusinessWeek* magazine named him one of the best managers of 2004. The magazine cited Immelt's drive to make GE a customer-driven, global company. And he had the tools, knowledge, and experience gained during almost twenty-five years at GE to guide him. So it's no wonder that total revenue at the company has increased $21 billion since 2002 (his first full year on the job) with earnings up $2.652 billion.

Bob Nardelli, CEO of Home Depot, was also named one of *BusinessWeek*'s best managers of 2004. Given how he started his tenure at Home Depot at the end of 2000, that's a remarkable accomplishment. Nardelli came out of the box swinging and immediately started looking for ways to cut expenses. Not knowing what he didn't know, he mandated that the stores increase the number of part-time sales clerks and cut knowledgeable full-time employees from the payroll. Faced with employees who couldn't answer basic home improvement questions, customers flocked to the competition, most notably Lowe's and same-store sales plummeted. The lessons Bob Nardelli had learned at GE about running efficient operations and using technology wisely helped him turn things around.

He knew it was critical to make Home Depot more efficient and make sure the shelves were stocked with merchandise customers wanted. To do that, he centralized buying, renovated dowdy stores, and invested in new technology, such as self-checkout lanes. For Nardelli, 2001 and 2002 were tough years, but he eventually learned what he didn't know. Home Depot is now the second-largest retailer in the United States, with 2005 revenues projected to reach $80 billon, right behind Wal-Mart. Bob Nardelli calls it the "sweetest spot in retailing."

After leaving GE, James McNerney became CEO of 3M on January 1, 2001. In a January 2001 interview in *Fortune* magazine, McNerney said,". . . I think marrying some of the GE culture with the already existing 3M culture can bear some fruit. It will still look more like the 3M culture than the GE culture, but there'll be some new elements." He couldn't have been more right. In his first four years on the job, McNerney has proven that some of the same management techniques that worked well at General Electric worked at 3M. He initiated the use of Six Sigma, a process that saves money by fixing manufacturing problems. He cut expenses (costs had been increasing twice as fast as the rate of sales) and established a company-wide leadership training program.

On McNerney's watch, net sales at 3M have increased from $16.7 billion to $20.0 billion. Net income went from $1.867 billion to $3.0 billion, an all-time high. McNerney's outstanding performance was recognized when he was named one of the best managers of 2003 by *BusinessWeek*.

McNerney's success can be attributed to his talent and the management knowledge he gained at GE. He had worked in lighting, electrical, financial services, and the aircraft engine business and had headed GE's operations in Asia for two years. When he moved from one manufacturing conglomerate to another he knew the right questions to ask based on his previous experience. As Edward Brennan, a 3M board member and former chairman of Sears said, "It was as close to a perfect fit as one could find."

Now, consider the story of Larry Johnston, CEO of Albertson's Inc., the supermarket and drugstore chain with almost $40 billion in revenue and 2,500 stores. Johnston joined Albertson's in April 2001. He thought the knowledge he acquired during his twenty-nine-year career at General Electric would help him lead Albertson's in the highly competitive grocery business. According to a May 15, 2002, article in *The Wall Street Journal,* some employees complained that he relied on his GE experience too often. "I don't care," Johnston was quoted as saying. "It's what I know best."

Following the General Electric mantra of being Number one or Number two in a business, Johnston has pulled Albertson's completely out of markets where the company is unable to compete. He's emphasized upgrading technology and instituted a new national advertising campaign, "Working hard to make our customers' lives easier."

What Johnston hasn't been able to do is find Albertson's sweet spot against the competition, especially the Wal-Mart powerhouse. Gary Giblen, director of research for C.L. King Associates, an independent stock research firm, sees Albertson's lack of distinctive market positioning as a negative. "It's not the leader in price, service, or assortment, and the stores are still plain vanilla and don't have much resonance with consumers." And David Pinto in a *Chain Drug Review* article said that there is an answer to Albertson's lack of direction and dismal financial results, including declining same-store sales: "When it comes to transferring success from one business segment to another, commitment to and knowledge of the business is at least as important as leadership and management ability."

The moral of this tale? Critical success factors are different for each company. What was critical for a company like General Electric wasn't even on the radar for a company like Albertson's. Managers and executives who move from one company to another and from one industry to another need to know what they don't know and learn to ask the right questions of the right people. If they do this, they can discover the critical success factors that can propel their company to increased sales and sustained profitability. If they don't, they might set their company on a path toward bankruptcy.

When Board Members Don't Know They Don't Know

What do a retired executive in the entertainment and communications business, the CEO of a national publications distribution company, a restaurant executive, and the former CEO of a chemical and plastics manufacturer have in common? No, this isn't the beginning of a joke. These four people were actually on the board of directors of Kmart in the years immediately before the company declared Chapter 11. Without retail experience, they didn't know the unknown unknowns—the critical issues that Kmart was facing. So they didn't know the right questions to ask when they were considering hiring Chuck Conaway as CEO.

I believe Chuck took the job with the best intentions of making Kmart into a viable company. Unfortunately, neither Conaway nor the board of directors realized that he didn't know what he didn't know. Chuck came from CVS, a regional drugstore chain, where he was the president and COO and was in charge of marketing, operations, and technology. He knew nothing about most of Kmart's businesses, but his successes at CVS gave him—and Kmart's board— the false confidence to believe that he could successfully run a mass retailer. So when Conaway presented his rather dramatic plan to increase sales, the uninformed board rubber-stamped it. Eighteen months later, Kmart was in bankruptcy court.

Floyd Hall, former chairman and chief executive of Kmart, said he "absolutely" and "wholeheartedly" finds the board of directors responsible for Kmart's bankruptcy. "I don't think they knew enough about the business to really see Chuck's lack of experience," Hall said in an April 5, 2003, article in *Free Business Press*. When the company exited bankruptcy, the board that hired Conaway was replaced with nine new directors, heavily weighted with current or retired investment professionals.

Sadly, this is far from an isolated situation. Boards of directors are often composed of people with little or no experience in a particular industry. And they're expected to leverage that lack of knowledge to guide their companies through the challenges they face.

Even Doctors Don't Know What They Don't Know

In 1976, people in Connecticut began appearing in doctors' offices with symptoms that could not be identified with an existing disease. This illness, transmitted by a tick, was eventually named Lyme disease. Although incidences of this disease increased, most doctors were not aware of its existence. They didn't know what they didn't know. This lack of information had dire consequences for Richard Gerstner, a rising executive at IBM, who some said was in line to become chairman of the company.

Starting in 1987, Gerstner was struck with a number of physical problems. Doctors were not able to pinpoint exactly what was causing his symptoms. Finally in 1989, unable to contend with the pain from his ailments, he resigned from IBM. After seeing a number of specialists and having two back operations, Gerstner was no better. In February 1992, his wife had a chance encounter with the wife of another IBM employee. Mary Joette Gerstner recounted her husband's symptoms. She then learned from the woman, who had been diagnosed with Lyme disease, that her husband probably had the same disease. A new doctor accurately diagnosed Gerstner's Lyme disease and put him on antibiotics. Gerstner recovered and by 1993 was ready to go back to work. To Gerstner's chagrin, his brother, Louis, was named chairman of IBM. Unable to return to IBM after his recovery, Richard Gerstner went on to become the president and CEO of Telular Corporation, a wireless communication company, and is now the owner of his own financial consulting firm.

Richard Gerstner lived in Connecticut and vacationed on Long Island where Lyme disease was prevalent. Yet no doctor knew about or thought to test for the disease. So the doctors' lack of knowledge, the unknown unknowns about Lyme disease, cost Gerstner his career at IBM.

To sum this up, while having relevant experience is certainly a desirable quality in a manager or executive, it's not 100 percent required. The trick is to make sure that if you don't know what you need to know, you surround yourself with people who do. These people can come from inside or outside your organization—just be careful whom you ask. All too frequently, we go to the people least equipped to help us: our colleagues. Many of these people work in the same company or industry, have similar backgrounds and similar experiences. Very often they provide the comfort of having the same opinion and reinforce our "good judgment."

My good friend and mentor Jim Posner, a founder of Home Decorators Collection, is a classic example of the importance of knowing where to get the knowledge he doesn't have. Home Decorators Collection is a business that has a great catalog filled with all sorts of furniture, rugs, lamps, and other household furnishings. When Jim and his business partners started the company, none of them knew very much about the furniture business, but they knew about catalogs. So they formed alliances with furniture experts (mostly manufacturers) from all over the world. They gave these experts space in the catalog to fill up any way they wanted. Each edition of the catalog goes out to 16 million people. Customers then vote by buying or not buying what's on those pages. The company tracks the sales of every single item on every page, and the ones that don't sell are out of the next issue. So a critical success factor for HDC is to find suppliers who have products that their core customers want to buy.

After all is said and done, you absolutely must understand your business. Warren Buffett, who knows a thing or two about running successful businesses, has repeatedly said that he only invests in businesses and stocks of companies he understands. Buffett has been quoted as saying, "Figure out what business you understand and concentrate." And also, "What I like is economic strength in an area where I understand it and where I think it will last." Warren Buffett knows what's right.

B2B: Helping Your Customers Find Their Critical Success Factors

If you're in a B2B situation, it's important that your customers identify their critical success factors. If they don't, identifying your own will be nearly impossible. One of my clients operated call centers and was hired by big magazine publishers to call people whose subscriptions were expiring and ask them to renew. His company received a flat amount per hour and he paid his telesalespeople the same way. On average, each salesperson renewed one subscription per hour.

Here's where things got a little sticky. The more subscriptions a magazine has, the more it can charge for advertising, which is where most of their revenue comes from. That made renewing subscriptions a critical success factor for the publishers—and for my client. Increasing each salesperson's renewal rate from one to two, or even 1.5, would have a huge impact on the publishers' and my client's businesses.

Recognizing that, he tried to change the compensation from a flat rate to a pay-for-performance program based on hitting certain renewal-rate targets. That would have enabled him to pass those incentives on to his staff, which would have undoubtedly increased the sales-per-hour figure. But the publishers didn't seem to care about any of that—they just wanted my client to "burn through the list"; in other words, call everyone, ask them to renew, and move on to the next one.

Not understanding how important getting renewals

were caused the publishers to see this program as an expense rather than a critical success factor. When business got tough and something had to go, guess which program was cut? Because of this burn-the-list perspective, the publishers lost subscriptions, which led to reduced advertising revenue, which forced an expense cutback, which reduced the renewal program. Do the words "death spiral" come to mind?

Keep Looking: The Critical Success Factors May Be Right in Front of You

It's amazing what you can learn when you take the time to listen carefully. I recently took a trip to the Henry Doorly Zoo in Omaha, Nebraska, with my son, daughter-in-law, and two-and-a-half-year-old grandchild. If you've never been to this zoo and you get to Omaha, don't miss it. Truly one of the greatest zoos in the country.

As we were walking through the new gorilla house, we talked about how amazing it was that a community the size of Omaha could raise the kind of money it took to build such a wonderful facility. My daughter-in-law had just visited Zoo Atlanta, which wasn't even in the same league as Omaha's. We wondered why Atlanta, Georgia, with the population and wealth it has, couldn't afford better. After some conversation, the answer was quite simple. Dr. Lee Simmons, the director of the Henry Doorly Zoo, is an innovator, a leader, and a motivator. He's been able to muster the forces of the Omaha community to support the zoo. Many of Omaha's successful individuals and businesses have freely given money to make it one of the top zoos in the United States. There is no question that Atlanta has greater financial resources, but unfortunately, the city has never been able to motivate the community to support a facility comparable to Omaha's.

So the great lesson from this conversation was the difference between what's important—like money—and what's critical to success—leadership and vision. And that is why a city the size of Omaha has a greater zoo than a city the size of Atlanta.

Putting It All Together

You've focused on *what's* right instead of *who's* right, dug deeper into the data you already have, asked the right people, avoided the temptation to build consensus, and you know what you don't know. Congratulations! Now you have all the information you need to write down the two or three ideas that are critical to your company's success.

Your critical success factors will be specific to your company and you'll have to choose them carefully. Critical success factors must also be SMART: specific, measurable, accountable, realistic, and time bound. This means that specific goals must be established, progress reports must be made on a regular basis, and the goals held as absolutes. By focusing on what's critical to your company's success, your management and employees will always know exactly what needs to be accomplished to reach the objectives.

One person has to be responsible for making sure the objectives related to the critical success factors are being met. A regular review process must be established and its performance made a priority. If the critical success factors are not being met, you need to find out why and make the necessary adjustments immediately. Your goals might be unrealistic or the critical success factors might not be precise enough.

Now it's time to make sure you are hiring must-have employees—the right people for the right jobs—who can be successful in your company's unique environment. We'll talk about exactly that in the next chapter.

STEP 6

Must-Have Employees

Throughout this book I've talked about a number of different kinds of customers:

- Core customers. The 20 percent of your base that contributes 80 percent of the profits. The kind of customers you wish you had more of.
- Opportunistic customers. The 80 percent of your base that often costs you more to service than they contribute to your bottom line.
- Must-have customers. Potential customers who look a lot like your core customers, but they're

someone else's core customers. These are the people you need to be doing business with if you're going to prosper.

The reason I'm bringing all this up again is that everything I've said about customers can be applied to employees, as well.

- Core employees. The kind of employees you wish you had more of. They're loyal, they go the extra mile without being asked.
- Opportunistic employees. The kind of employee you wish you'd never hired. They aren't loyal to your company, they do the minimum required to collect their paycheck, and would jump to another employer in a heartbeat if they had a better offer.
- Must-have employees. Potential employees who look a lot like your core employees, with all the characteristics you're looking for. Only problem is that they're currently working for someone else.

As with customers, for your business to thrive, you'll need to increase the percentage of core employees and decrease the percentage of opportunistic ones. And the way to do that is to identify and attract your must-have employees.

Identifying Your Core and Must-Have Employees

Identifying your core employees is a relatively straightforward process—it's all about shared values. To a great extent, these values are the same ones you share with your core and must-have customers. If you value quality, customer service, reliability, or whatever, your core employees do, too. And so do your must-have employees.

John E. Anderson, PhD, is the founder and chairman of the Center for Sports Psychology. He advises the U.S. Olympic team and business executives on a concept he calls organizational relationship. According to Anderson, people form relationships with the organizations they work for, as well as the people they interact with. If an individual's attitudes and values match those of the organization, the individual can perform at peak capacity. If those values don't mesh, performance is less than optimal.

To illustrate his point, Anderson cites winners of the 2004 NBA Championship (Detroit Pistons) and the 2004 Super Bowl (New England Patriots). What separated those two teams from their rivals was that they each placed a very high value on teamwork. Yes, both teams had some stars, but they weren't show-cased, and the emphasis was on the team as a whole. At the Super Bowl, the Patriots took the very unusual step of being introduced as a team instead of as individuals. And in the NBA, the Pistons felt that adding a marquee name would have disrupted their organization and cost them the championship. The team they beat, the Los Angeles Lakers, however, were dominated by two highly paid and highly touted superstars, Shaquille O'Neal and Kobe Bryant.

Sports teams are like every other business, small or large. If your employees' values aren't aligned with those of the rest of your organization, you'll have a tough time winning any big games. But if you and your employees share the same values, you're guaranteed to succeed.

Playing by Your Rules

We've already talked about the rules you have for your customers. As you might expect, the same goes for employees. The rules aren't as simple as "make your sales quota," or "you've missed too many meetings." The rules are a reflection of your values.

When you're making hiring decisions, employees' and prospective employees' values are often more important than other seemingly important characteristics, such as education, years of experience, or where a person's worked before.

Let's say your company provides janitorial and cleaning services for buildings and homes. If you were looking to increase your staff, chances are you'd try to hire people with a lot of cleaning experience.

You'd put ads in the paper that stressed cleaning experience, you'd screen applicants for experience, and you'd end up with a short list of people you'd want to interview. Unfortunately, if you went through this process—which nearly every company does—you'd miss some of the best people.

When it comes right down to it, experience in cleaning is a nice thing, but what you really want is people who have a real passion for it, the kind of people who straighten pictures when they walk into a room, people who won't let you put a drink on their coffee table without a coaster. I'll talk about how you go about finding people with a passion for what you do in a minute, but first let me give you a couple of real-life examples.

At Best Buy, some of their new sales associates have a lot of experience selling computer products. But that's frosting on the cake. Best Buy really wants to hire people who share the company's values, who are passionate about the products and services Best Buy sells. Most newly hired associates were regular customers who really loved the stores. Another trait that Best Buy looks for is the ability to teach and share knowledge with others, to take complex ideas and make them easier to understand. Those traits wouldn't show up in most want ads, but they're values that are absolutely central to Best Buy. Those are Best Buy's rules.

Starbucks has some pretty clear rules, too. I asked Ron Weber, a buyer at Starbucks, to tell me about the values they look for in their employees. Here's what he said: "Bright, energetic, creative, diverse people from all backgrounds are welcome. We want people who are customer-focused, project-oriented, work hard, have fun, enjoy teamwork, and value people, families, communities, and the environment. We want them to treat others with respect and dignity. Retail and/or food and beverage experience is a plus." Did you notice that the job experience rule was all the way at the end? Actually, it isn't even a rule at all. Relevant experience might get you a job interview, but it won't get you the job.

MicroTek is another company that has clearly defined rules. In case you've never heard of them, MicroTek is "a training facilities and event logistics provider." They provide computer-equipped classroom facilities and meeting rooms to companies to conduct training. They provide reservations tracking, technical support, catering, and amenities—everything the customer needs to conduct a successful training event.

When I asked Don Slivensky, MicroTek's CEO, he told me that the company values hospitality and a strong work ethic. They want people who will apply a sense of ownership to their responsibilities, and in turn feel a sense of loyalty and accomplishment with the ongoing success of the company. Most important, though, they want people who share the company's value of always being willing to go the extra mile to provide what he called "outrageous customer service." Slivensky gave me some great examples: changing a student's flat tire, dog-sitting an instructor's dog, and accommodating clients' special dietary needs.

Lincoln Plating looks for people with talent who will recognize and seek multiple responsibilities in their jobs. Successful employees have a desire for newness and change and look forward to the next project. Lincoln's adviser on organizational alignment, John Anderson, whom you read about in the beginning of this chapter, told me that if someone's orientation is to do the same job every day, he or she is simply not going to work out. People with a single job orientation are a better fit at another company. Lincoln Plating's commitment to their employees has been recognized nationally. In 2004 and 2005 the Society for Human Resource Management recognized the company as one of the 25 best medium-size companies to work for in America.

One particularly values-driven company is Chick-fil-A, whose founder, S. Truett Cathy, requires that every store close on Sundays. For Cathy, Sunday is "a very special day, a divine day, a day that is set aside for family and to worship, if you choose." The "never on Sunday" policy has helped Chick-fil-A attract franchisees and employees who appreciate Sunday off, whether they go to church or not. According to Truett Cathy, in most cases, a Chick-fil-A restaurant generates more revenue in six days than their competitors do in seven.

Chick-fil-A also has a strong commitment to community involvement. And they sell franchises only to people who feel the same way and who are from the community where the store will be located. The company's pickiness is legendary. In 2003, over ten thousand people applied to be Chick-fil-A restaurant operators. The company accepted only ninety-two.

So how can you tell whether your core and must-have employees share your company's values? Before you can answer that question, everyone in your organization has to be absolutely clear on what your values are. That clarity may help you avoid some costly mistakes.

Almost everyone wants to hire the best and the brightest—or at least they think they do. Quite often they're wrong. My company was once hired by a national department store chain to help them identify why more than half of the three hundred bright young college recruits that they brought in every year left within two years. The company spent a lot of money sending recruiters to visit college campuses, identifying top performers, wining and dining them, hiring them, and finally training them. But sure as clockwork, within twenty-four months, more than 150 of them would be gone.

It took us just a few visits to figure out exactly what the problem was. To sum it up, the company had an unwritten rule that all these bright young people needed to check their brains at the door. They weren't paid to think; they were paid to do. The company had a rigid set of policies and processes and new employees were expected to toe the line. So after a while, the creative thinkers couldn't stand it anymore and left.

I'm not making any judgments here about whether valuing creative thinking is a good thing or a bad thing. In fact, there are plenty of jobs where creativity isn't necessary or even desirable. The point here is that you need to be sure that everyone in your organization agrees on what your values are. Remember the car example from Chapter 2? In this case, the HR department saw the company as a Corvette, but the CEO was thinking pickup truck.

So ask yourself this: Would I rather kick a mule or rein in a stallion? The mule is nonthreatening and easy to live with. The stallion has a mind of his own and gets things done. In some companies mules are preferred because they follow instructions and play by the rules. In others it's all about stallions: Give them some general guidelines and get out of their way. In a company of stallions, mules get trampled. In a company of mules, stallions are a pain in the mule.

How Do You Identify Shared Values?

Okay, now let's get back to the all-important issues of identifying shared values and finding people with a passion for what your company does. There are a number of excellent ways.

- **Ask your core employees what they value most about working for your company.** At Micro-Tek, employees overwhelmingly say they stick around because they feel valued and they know that every MicroTek employee is important to the success of the company. They say they're grateful for the autonomy that they have in their positions, and they know their suggestions on any topic are always welcome. They've seen Micro-Tek take care of the employees in times of need, and that has inspired great loyalty. There is a true sense of family, of camaraderie, of caring and generosity. Above all else, they are proud of the work that MicroTek does and they're glad to be a part of it.

- **Ask your core customers what they value most about your employees.**
- **Ask your core employees to recommend people to fill your job vacancies.**
- **Get your core employees involved in the interviewing and hiring process.** They'll have a much better sense of whether everyone clicks or not.
- **Ask prospective employees the right questions.** Although I've put it last, this is a critical step. By carefully designing the questions you ask during job interviews, you can greatly improve the odds that the people you hire will turn out to be core employees and not opportunistic ones. For example, have questions that encourage candidates to talk about how passionate they are about your company and/or your products.

When Starbucks asks a future employee why he or she wants to work at the company, they aren't necessarily waiting to hear someone say, "I love coffee!" People aren't required to drink coffee or even like coffee to work at Starbucks. Management is looking for employees who have a passion for the way Starbucks does business.

- At Harrah's, everyone who comes in for an interview spends a few hours going through a proprietary assessment that's designed to identify people who are likely to succeed.
- MicroTek uses specially written interview guides that focus on teamwork, creativity, integrity, related skills, motivation, and leadership.

There are a number of excellent companies out there that can structure selection interviews to assist you in finding more people like your very best. When you're interviewing potential suppliers, make sure you're very clear on what the interviews are designed to identify. Interviews range in quality, complexity, and cost from very simple paper-and-pencil and web-based interviews, to more sophisticated telephone interviews with trained analysts. Some are good for identifying basics like friendliness, work ethic, and honesty, while others can predict with reasonable accuracy the success of a future CEO or president.

When a Value Isn't a Value: Putting the Right People in the Right Job

Don Clifton, the late chairman of the Gallup Organization, was one of the most gifted people analyzers I've ever known. Don's legacy was teaching the world about people's unique strengths. His teachings have helped millions achieve personal and professional success. One of his favorite sayings was, You can't teach a pig to sing. It frustrates you and annoys the pig. What Don meant was that every single person you walk by on the street has his or her strengths. Not every employee is a good fit in every company. The right person in the right job is a formula for superior performance and superior results. But putting the same "right" person in the wrong job is like trying to teach a pig to sing.

Think about Michael Jordan. On the basketball court, Jordan was the best in the world. On the baseball diamond, though, he was good but not good enough to make it out of the minor leagues. In this case, the issue was that despite being a marvelously gifted athlete, Jordan simply lacked the skills to excel in baseball. The same, of course, can happen in business. (In Chapter 5, we talked about how well—or not so well—a CEO's skill set can transfer between industries.)

Putting employees in an environment where they can thrive is a question of shared values. And it's critical to understand that values that are important in one company may not be relevant in another. Take Michael Frances, the executive vice president of marketing for Target Corporation, and one of the great retail marketers of all time. Michael has a license to do almost anything as long as it supports Target's positioning by projecting an upbeat, contemporary, leading-edge fashion image that communicates with a very specific must-have customer. He continuously wins awards for creativity and a paradigm-breaking approach to customer communication.

Now imagine Michael moving from a great organization like Target to another great organization like Wal-Mart. Both companies are in the discount store business, but in very different ways. Wal-Mart's advertising and communication are low budget, middle of the road, and continuously focus on the message of "low price always." That approach is absolutely perfect for Wal-Mart. But what do you think would happen if Michael Frances took a job at Wal-Mart, where he'd be creatively limited? To start with, he'd be miserable and frustrated. As a result, he wouldn't be able to produce the kind of work and project the kind of image that Wal-Mart values. What a waste of a great talent.

When you hire the right people for your business model, your company can soar to new heights and reach its goals. In my twenty-six years in business and fifteen years as a consultant, I've seen numerous promising business plans or projects torpedoed by having the wrong person in the wrong job. And I've seen companies brought to the brink of extinction—and sometimes driven over the brink—because the wrong person was leading the charge. I've also seen companies completely revitalized when management is dedicated to hiring the right people for every job.

As a boys' apparel buyer, Bob Rowan was consistently one of the most profitable merchants in my company. He was so successful that we put him in charge of buying for the young men's department. A few months after Bob took over his new position, our director of human resources told me that Bob was failing in this new position and would need to be terminated. I visited with Bob to find out what was wrong. He hated this new position. On the surface, the two departments seemed very similar. But in practice, boys' apparel was a very basic, predictable business, while young men's was fast-changing and unpredictable.

I'd worked with Bob for many years and didn't want to let him go. So I asked him what job he'd like if he could pick any one in the company. His face lit up, and he said he'd love to be a sporting goods apparel buyer. He loved sports. The business was predictable and didn't change much from season to season. I moved Bob out of young men's apparel and into sporting goods. Two years later he was named merchant of the year, earned a bonus equal to double his salary, and got a free trip to Hawaii for himself and his wife. When he became the right person in the right position, he achieved excellence.

As I mentioned above, there are many companies that can help you structure job interviews. Similarly, there are quite a few vendors who offer interviews and tests designed to put the right person in the right job *after* he or she has already been hired. As you might expect, some systems are better than others. Some produce excellent results, while others don't provide enough critical information for you to make an informed choice. When interviewing vendors—and I strongly suggest you talk with at least three—only consider those with a proven track record in putting the right people in the right job.

Employee Loyalty

In Chapter 4, we talked about the huge difference between satisfied customers and loyal customers. As you might expect, almost everything that we talked about with regard to customer loyalty applies to employee loyalty, as well. When your employees are satisfied, you're meeting their expectations and not mistreating them. But you're also not doing anything to keep them from taking a hike if they get a better offer somewhere else.

Almost every company in every industry measures employee turnover. In the retail industry, for example, it's not unusual for turnover to run between 100 and 120 percent annually (meaning that some positions turn over more than once per year). A lot of managers and executives aren't bothered at all by those numbers. Their philosophy is that turnover is actually a good thing because it allows the company to lower its costs by getting rid of high-earning employees and bringing in lower-earning ones.

Underestimating or ignoring the true costs of turnover is a colossal mistake. According to HR.com, a human resources Web site, it costs two to three times more to replace a worker than to keep an existing one. But that's not all. A few years ago, the Harvard Business School conducted an in-depth study on the real cost of turnover and found the true cost of replacing an employee is 1.6 times his or her annual salary. Other organizations have put the cost at two to three times the annual salary. This includes obvious direct costs, such as recruiting and retraining, and less obvious, indirect costs, such as decreased customer service, lost customers and sales, and decreased productivity.

What does this mean to you? Let's assume you pay your employees an average annual salary of $70,000, and you lose ten people per year. Even using Harvard's low-end number, turnover costs you over $1.1 million every year. Have I got your attention?

Not surprisingly, there's a measurable correlation between employee loyalty and customer loyalty. According to Janet Kraus, CEO of Circles, a provider of loyalty management solutions, "Customer loyalty and employee loyalty are interrelated in ways that directly affect the profitability of the business relationship. . . . When you look at the companies that are on the lists of the best places to work—Southwest Airlines, Lands' End, Harley-Davidson—these are the same companies that are considered to be leaders in customer service."

The Container Store is consistently rated as one

of the hundred best places to work. What sets The Container Store apart from most other retailers is its consummate attention to customer service and its commitment to its employees. Read the company's Web site, and you'll learn that "employees are recognized as the company's greatest asset," "one of The Container Store's core business philosophies is that one great person equals three good people," and "at The Container Store, service equals selling."

The privately held company, with thirty-three stores, sells a vast selection of storage and organizational products. Yearly sales were about $310 million in 2003 and the company has an average annual sales growth of 20 to 25 percent. The company, founded in 1978, has been in the top three in *Fortune* magazine's annual list of 100 Best Companies to Work For from 2000 to 2004. So you can see, based on the numbers, The Container Store is a prime example of a company that hires people who will produce superior results within its business model.

To quantify this, consider a major study done with a

national food chain, by Harvard B-school professors James Heskett, Earl Sasser, and Leonard Schlesinger. They found that stores in the top 20 percent for employee retention were 55 percent more profitable than stores in the bottom 20 percent.

The Right People Equals the Right Results

Take a look at the chart below, which compares Costco with Sam's Club, Wal-Mart's warehouse/outlet division. Costco focuses on hiring the right people for its fast-paced, physically active environment. When Costco finds the right people, they pay them 35 percent more than Sam's. And 82 percent of Costco employees are covered by the company's health plan, versus only 47 percent at Sam's. Not surprisingly, Costco beats Sam's on every measure of productivity and has a turnover rate that's less than a third of Sam's.

	Costco	**Sam's**
Employee turnover	6%	21%
Labor and overhead costs	9.8% of sales	17% of sales
Sales per square foot	$795	$516
Profits per employee	$13,647	$11,039
Yearly operating income growth	10.1%	9.8%

It's Not All About Money

As important as pay and benefits are, it turns out that a number of intangible benefits are far more important. In many companies, it's the environment and the company culture that turns talented, dedicated people into frustrated, poor performers. Manpower, the largest staffing and employment service in the world, surveyed 2,627 HR people in eight countries for the International Employee Loyalty 2002 study. The respondents considered the strongest drivers of employee loyalty as strong leadership, strong teamwork, employee recognition, and open/honest communication.

Having worked with companies across the country, I've seen that managers of the best, most profitable companies understand that they need to go beyond simply hiring the right people for the right positions. Employees also need an environment in which they can grow and thrive. They need to feel their opinion and input are important and that they are a vital member of the organization, no matter what their job. When this happens they are far more likely to arrive at work on time, be productive every day, and tell management when some process can be improved or when money can be saved. If employees feel that the company cares for them, they will care for the company. That's what fosters long-term dedication and loyalty.

Managing Turnover

I want you to take a short quiz that I call the cement truck test. It goes like this: What would happen if one of your great people, someone who plays a critical role in your company's success, was hit by a cement truck? Would your company still be successful? Succession planning is an important element in a company's long-range planning. However, in today's business climate, most companies are lean and mean. Management finds the time and money to think about all the catastrophes that can negatively affect a business *except* the loss of a key player. This means the company is covered for fire, liability, and business interruption insurance, but not if a valuable executive is hit by a cement truck.

Unfortunately, few companies have the right people backing up their critical players. Is there a difference between insurance on tangible assets and a sound succession plan? Is losing your superstar sales manager any less of a loss than losing a plant to a fire? In one of my early consulting projects I was asked to turn around a five-million-dollar company that went from a two-million-dollar profit to a two-million-dollar loss in two years after the manager left. Your succession plan may be more critical than your insurance coverage.

When you are putting together a succession plan, always put the shared values and strengths of each individual first, and his or her work experience second—or maybe even third. In most organizations, bright, talented people who share your values and passion can learn the tactical aspects of a position in a relatively short time.

Of course, not every key player you lose will leave in a hearse. Some valuable employees will just quit and go somewhere else. Whenever that happens, try to find out why. How? Ask. Could be health reasons, marriage, divorce, moving out of the area, and so on. But it could also be something else, such as a change in your company's culture, policies, or procedures. Losing great people, regardless of the reason, is a great loss, and every executive should be responsible and accountable for managing that kind of turnover.

Creating an Environment that Breeds Success

Knowing your employees' rules—what's critical to them and exactly what you have to do to meet their needs—is the key to attracting and keeping loyal employees. If you aren't 100 percent sure what their rules are, your core employees will be glad to tell you.

But they won't say anything unless you ask them. You'd think that would be simple enough, but it's amazing how many otherwise intelligent managers never bother to ask their core employees anything at all, or who go through the motions by buying an employee satisfaction survey from the lowest bidder and distributing it to everyone in the company. And they get what they paid for: Most of the time these surveys provide information that's nice to know as opposed to insights that can be the basis for meaningful internal change.

With a little extra effort, you can get an employee survey that's worth more than the paper it's printed on. Given that payroll is most companies' biggest expense, a properly thought-out and executed survey will pay for itself a hundred times over in increased productivity and sales.

In an article in the *Harvard Business Review,* Palmer Morrel-Samuels, a research psychologist, explained how companies can benefit from good quality workplace surveys and questionnaires. A study done by GTE in the mid-1990s revealed that the performance of its different billings operations, as measured by the accuracy of bills sent out, was closely tied to the leadership style of the unit managers. The company encouraged changes in leadership style through training sessions, discussion groups, and videos. In the year following the survey, GTE showed a 22 percent increase in billing accuracy, and another 24 percent the year after that.

The best employee survey I know of was developed by the Gallup Organization, based on their interviews with over a million employees over a twenty-five-year period. The Gallup survey is a deceptively simple list of twelve questions that very accurately gauge a company's ability to motivate and retain employees who will produce superior results.

The questions include:

- Do I know what is expected of me at work?
- Do I have the materials and equipment I need to do my work right?
- At work, do I have the opportunity to do what I do best every day?
- In the last seven days, have I received recognition or praise for doing good work?

- Does my supervisor, or someone at work, seem to care about me as a person?

When your employees can reply yes to these five questions and the other seven, you know you've created a truly motivational environment. (For an in-depth discussion of all of Gallup's twelve questions, I highly recommend *First, Break All the Rules* by Marcus Buckingham and Curt Coffman.)

Learning to Ask the Right People the Right Questions

Your employees know more than you do. They're on the front lines every day, dealing with your customers and the inner workings of the company. Your employees know better than you do what's causing the problems that cost you sales, reduce quality and productivity, and lead to employee dissatisfaction, which itself results in poor customer service. And they'll tell you if you ask. The right way.

To start with, you've got to ask the right people. I can't emphasize this enough: If you want accurate, actionable information, you must ask only your core employees. Anything anyone else has to say is worthless. Second, you have to ask the right questions. The typical question managers pose—Are you satisfied?—generally yields superficial answers, like "sure," or "everything's fine." It's just as productive as asking your teenager how school was ("fine") or where he or she is going ("out").

Instead, start asking your core employees the Gallup questions I listed on page 241; and add the following:

- If you could make any change to improve our company, what is the one change you would make?
- If we only have one additional dollar to spend next year, what should we spend it on?
- Do you know why our best customers buy from us?
- Why do customers stop doing business with us?
- If we wanted to destroy the company, what is the one thing we should stop doing?

The Benefits

These questions are extremely powerful, and the information they yield can turn your business around. A few years ago, I conducted an employee survey for a very successful company that wasn't performing up to capacity. Turnover was high and worker productivity was low. Most of the responses indicated a reasonable level of satisfaction throughout the organization. Employees were generally happy with their pay and benefits. Most people liked the physical environment and, for the most part, they felt that they had the equipment they needed. But when asked, If you could make any change to improve our company, what is the one change you would make? a more serious problem was revealed.

In the company's most important department, 72 out of 126 people suggested replacing the executive vice president who headed this department. This response was unaided, and the way we administered the survey made it impossible for the employees to have planned this response as a group.

The CEO was shocked. This VP had worked for the organization for over twenty years, ran a critical part of the business, and was a personal friend of the CEO. The CEO chose not to make a personnel change despite the overwhelming feedback. The employees remained dissatisfied, turnover remained high, and productivity remained poor.

Another time, my company was called in by a regional newspaper chain for help on a similar high-turnover/low-productivity issue. In this case, it had to do with one specific department, the mail room, where retailers' color advertising was inserted into the newspapers before the papers were loaded onto distribution trucks. The department was in the basement in a vast sea of concrete with no windows and the thunder of the inserting machinery was nearly deafening. Employees in this area earned slightly more than minimum wage and worked from 11:00 P.M. to 7:00 A.M., 364 days a year.

Most of the workers staffed an eight-station circular machine that dropped copies of the color inserts into the newspaper. The job consisted of taking a pile of inserts off a pallet, dropping the irregularly stacked inserts into a machine that vibrated them to a uniform stack, placing the stack on the inserting machine, and watching the inserts drop into the papers. The most exciting part of the job was clearing jams. When one station jammed, it stopped the entire operation and seven other people had to stand around twiddling their thumbs while one employee reset his station.

I wanted to personally speak with the employees to get firsthand feedback on what was causing the high turnover. Two discussion groups were organized, one with that department's core employees, the other with opportunistic employees, the guys my client regretted having hired in the first place. These opportunistic employees regularly showed up late—if they showed up at all. I asked the two groups the questions outlined above.

The opportunistic group had little useful to say. They hated their jobs and couldn't wait to move to another company. They resented the attitude of the old-timers who gave them "lip" for not doing a better job. They had no idea why employee turnover was high, and they had no suggestions for increasing productivity in the mail room.

The core employees were very good at doing their jobs. When they vibrated a stack and loaded it on the machine, their stations never jammed. These guys cared about the newspaper and were proud of their superior job skills. They loved the part of their job that kept them physically active, moving inserts from the pallets to the machines. But they hated having to stand around at their positions watching the inserts or waiting for jams to be cleared. These core employees were angry about the inefficient way management had organized the work area, and they resented the poor quality of people being hired, their lack of commitment to the job, and the sloppy work they did.

After listening to the core employees vent their frustration, I asked them for solutions to the problems. The group believed they could put inserts into more papers in less time if the weak people were eliminated and the strong ones manned two stations each. Also, since the most frequent cause of jams was very lightweight paper, the core employees suggested that the newspaper begin printing inserts on heavier paper.

Armed with what seemed like a couple of very reasonable suggestions, I proposed that my client test them out for a few days. The core employees' recommendations turned out to be dead on. In fairly short order, my client reduced the mail room staff by half. Production increased dramatically and turnover was almost eliminated. My client gave the core employees a 50 percent pay raise and still saved 25 percent on total production costs. All of this was the direct result of having asked the right people the right questions.

Other Ways to Listen So Your Employees Will Talk

As I mentioned above, all employees—regardless of the job or their position in the company—want to feel that their opinions count. One of the best ways to show them is to reward them for coming up with ideas that improve the company.

When I was an executive in a regional department store chain, I started a program called Bright Ideas, which encouraged employees to submit money or timesaving ideas for consideration. We publicized the program on posters in break rooms and near time clocks, and we made special cards for submitting ideas. The program cost us almost nothing to run, but generated hundreds of amazing ideas and millions of dollars in savings.

One of the most memorable bright ideas came from the accounts payable department, which processed thousands of invoices every day and frequently had situations that required correspondence and vendor follow-up. Every time an invoice or documentation was copied, someone had to take the time to punch the pieces of paper to put into a notebook for tracking and later follow-up. One accounts payable clerk suggested that we buy copy paper that was already prepunched with three holes. This small change in the business eliminated sixty hours of payroll every week!

Although bright ideas programs don't require much money to get off the ground, they do require some careful thought and planning. If yours is going to be a success, you'll need to do all of the following:

- **Get buy-in from top management.** If they don't support the idea, it'll crash.
- **Tell employees what the program is all about.** Here's how Ron Weber of Starbucks explained

their program to me: "One of Starbucks' guiding principles is to recognize that profitability is essential to our future success. It is up to each one of us to look for ways to reduce waste and reduce costs whenever possible."

- **Stay true to your values.** As a socially and environmentally responsible company, Starbucks encourages employees to work together to decrease waste and increase recycling. Here are a few employee suggestions that Starbucks implemented, which reduced the company's "environmental footprint," and saved a lot of money in the process.
  - Reduced overall napkin size from twelve by seventeen inches to thirteen by thirteen inches
  - Reduced the thickness of trash bags from 1.5 millimeters to 1.2 millimeters
  - Reduced the size of gift tissue from twenty by twenty inches to twenty by eighteen inches
  - Increased use of postconsumer fiber in packaging used for Starbucks products
  - Recycled used coffee grounds in stores, and gave to customers for use as garden mulch
  - Created "green teams," groups of employees

at each store who work to increase recycling and reduce waste.

- **Recognize and reward bright ideas that save money, increase customer service, or improve efficiency.** The specific reward should depend on the significance of the idea and, more importantly, on the needs of the individual employee who came up with it. Some, of course, want money. Others, however, might prefer recognition in the company newsletter, a company-paid vacation, a day off, or even just a big cheer at the morning meeting.

- **Reply back timely to those who submit ideas, whether they get implemented or not.** Having a program that solicits and then ignores ideas is worse than not having a program at all.

- **Incorporate an anonymous reporting component into your program so employees can make less-than-positive comments and suggestions, as well.** If you're truly committed to letting your employees know that their opinions are valued, you need to hear the bad stuff as well as the good. Negative comments or suggestions aren't always going to be easy to read, but if they come from core employees, chances are they're important. And if something is important enough to write about, it undoubtedly is having an effect on your business.

You can encourage anonymous reporting in several ways. At MicroTek, they send out a blind survey that gives employees the opportunity to raise any issues they have. The responses are sent directly to the CEO, who reads every one, categorizes and summarizes the information, and distributes the results company-wide along with an explanation of any required action plan.

Starbucks has a 24/7 toll-free number where employees can report ethical, legal, or other sensitive issues.

Skip the Performance Reviews

Most companies do annual performance reviews of all their employees. In some cases, the review process is very positive and people come away with a clear idea of what they can do better to make themselves and the company great. Unfortunately, all too often, the annual review process is at best routine, and at worst unproductive, simply focusing on what people have done wrong. Employees walk away demoralized, worried about job security and thinking about updating their résumé.

A detailed discussion of how to structure a performance review is a topic that warrants its own book. But for now, simply make sure your review process is positive, motivational, and actually adds value.

One of the strong recommendations I make to all of my clients is that at least once a year managers prepare two lists. The first is a list of people whom you'd hire again. These are the people who excel in their positions, are efficient and productive, have a positive attitude, and share your organizations' values. They are the motivated employees who make your company profitable. In short, they're the people you simply can't afford to lose.

The second list contains the names of employees you wouldn't rehire. These are the people who don't share your company's values. They're in their positions because they don't have the courage to walk out and find another job, or because you haven't fired them. Once you've put this list together, you've got some work to do, so read on.

Make Someone Happy—Fire Him (or Her)

Most managers I know would put firing an employee high on their list of things they hate to do. But often, showing someone the door is the best thing for everyone. For instance, if you made a mistake and put the wrong person in the wrong job, he's going to be frustrated and unproductive. If you're able to find a more appropriate place in your organization where he can thrive, jump on it. But there are times when he'd be better off finding an organization that values what he has to offer.

Getting rid of total deadbeats is a lot easier. People who are unproductive, lack passion, call in sick a lot, have all sorts of unexplained absences, and spend most of their time complaining are like a drain on your organization. They drive away customers, detract from your company's success, and often decrease the morale of everyone around them. Firing people like this will have an immediate, positive effect on your organization.

The hardest people to fire are often the hardest to identify—and potentially the most damaging. Remember the Rhodes Furniture salespeople we talked about in Chapter 5, the ones who were putting in sixty hours a week and, even then, barely making their quota? Many had been doing that for years and years. Their coworkers liked them, they were fun to have around, and everyone thought they were hard workers. But no one really saw what a tremendous drain they were on the company.

Take a look around your company and you'll probably find that you've got at least a few employees like this, people who are doing okay or just hanging on. Is "okay" or "just hanging on" what you want for your company? Probably not. You can try to improve these people's performance by dragging them through a remedial review process so someone can tell them about the poor job they're doing. Or you can threaten to fire them unless they improve. Or you can try to force them to remake their skills and personality. But that gets us back to the "teaching pigs to sing" problem.

The most responsible and humane solution is to invite these employees to find a position at another organization that's more aligned with their skills and beliefs. Inaction by management is an action. By not responding to poor fits in an organization and keeping weak people on your payroll, you're jeopardizing your entire company. On the other hand, replacing noncontributing hangers-on with people whose values and work ethic are aligned with yours is the best thing you can do for your business.

Conclusion

You've hired the right people for your company and put them in the right jobs. They're eager to assist customers and make your company a success. Now it's time to show your must-have customers that when it comes to what they want, you're the only company they should be doing business with.

STEP 7

Are We Communicating Effectively with Our Must-Have Customers?

Every once in a while I hear a CEO or a manager quote the old saw about advertising: "I know half of our ads are working. Problem is I don't know which half." That line always gets a couple of knowing chuckles from anyone within earshot, but it always makes me cringe. Advertising that produces the desired results is 100 percent in the hands of the people who write the checks. And there's absolutely no reason—and no excuse—for having advertising that doesn't work.

That said, the fact remains that most advertising *doesn't* work. And the reason is pretty simple: People aren't crystal clear on what advertising is supposed to accomplish. Is it supposed to make more people aware of the brand? Win awards for creativity? Increase sales? Well, let me clear things up right now. The goal of advertising is to:

- Give your core customers a reason to keep buying from you
- Give your must-have customers a reason to start buying from you
- Increase your sales and profits

That's it. Any advertising that doesn't achieve those three goals isn't really advertising. It's throwing money out the window. Unfortunately, in too many companies, the stuff that's being called advertising is really *egotising*—lovely little campaigns that win awards and make management feel good, but don't have any effect at all on sales or profits. Take a minute and think about your own advertising. Have you slipped into doing egotising? Here's how you can tell:

- The boys (or girls) at the club love it.
- Your ad agency wins an award.
- Your mother-in-law hates it (she's usually right).
- Your number of core customers is not growing.
- Your sales trend isn't changing.

I've promised my wife that in my next life I'm coming back as an advertising malpractice attorney. I want to help companies recover the money they wasted on advertising that either didn't help or actually did serious damage. Fortunately, I've got a plan in *this* life that will help you get the most out of your advertising.

Before we go on, though, I want to make sure that you understand how I'm using the term "advertising." Like it or not, planned or not, you have a brand. When people hear your company's name, they relate the name to a set of attributes they have stored in their minds. They believe your products are desirable or not, high quality or not, well styled or not, expensive or fair and so on. So advertising or communication becomes everything you do that includes your name. It's TV, radio, Internet, magazines and newspapers, public relations, corporate sponsorships, the décor of your stores, discount coupons, slotting fees, customer service, and just about anything else that has your name on it.

Okay, back to business.

You Get What You Bait For

As with everything else in this book, you have no business even thinking about spending money on advertising unless you know who your core and must-have customers are. I know, you'd think that would be a pretty basic thing. But you'd be amazed at the number of companies that spend millions on advertising to the wrong people.

On a recent trip to London, I spent forty-five minutes in line waiting to clear customs at Heathrow Airport. I'd already finished my book on the plane, so I spent the time checking out billboards in the terminal. Right away, the familiar face of Tiger Woods caught my eye. Instead of pitching golf clubs or even Buicks, Tiger was promoting Accenture Consulting with the tagline "Be a Tiger." I'm guessing that "Be a Tiger" was supposed to be a clever way of telling people that hiring Accenture would make you a winner like Tiger Woods. That's a reasonable point, I suppose. But with whom is Accenture trying to communicate?

Accenture is a high-end consulting firm and their core and must-have customers are very large corporations. All are well aware of Accenture. So what was the intent of this humongous billboard looming over the customs line at Heathrow? Could it have been to remind must-have customers that Accenture is out there and to drop their current consulting firm? Could it have been to encourage current clients to do more business with Accenture? I've worked with hundreds of CEOs and managers in my time and I can tell you that none of them would make a decision to hire—or do more business with—a consulting firm based on a billboard in an airport, especially one with such a sophomoric tag line.

So why spend the money on billboards? I really have no idea, and I'll bet Accenture doesn't, either. But my best guess is that the Tiger Woods campaign was a classic example of egotising. I'm sure that many Accenture execs are avid golfers, who jumped at the chance to hang out a little and pick up some tips from one of the best in the world. The fact that the ads were a waste of good paper probably never crossed their mind.

In Denver, near where I live, there are a number of stores that sell audio and video equipment, including Ultimate Electronics and Best Buy. Ultimate, as I talked about in Chapter 2, specializes in high-end brands, while Best Buy is far more mass market. There should be very little overlap when it comes to their core and must-have customers. Ultimate wants to reach audiophiles and videophiles who want top-of-the-line products and are willing to pay a premium for them. Best Buy wants to reach a larger, more budget-oriented crowd. So can anyone explain to me why both of these companies advertise in the Denver *Post,* and why their ads are almost identical?

The *Post* is probably a pretty good venue for Best Buy. But for Ultimate? I doubt that any more than 10 percent of the *Post*'s readers are Ultimate's must-have customers, which means that 90 percent of whatever they're paying for those ads is wasted. Wait, it gets worse. Ultimate's ads are filled with discount merchandise and individual components. But Ultimate's must-have customers are looking for something else entirely: high-end systems, which they'd never know Ultimate has because the ads don't give them a reason to go shopping. Conversely, mass-market consumers who visit an Ultimate store will find only a few budget items and premium equipment that they probably perceive as overpriced, and will leave without buying a thing. Given all that, the percentage of Ultimate's wasted ad spending goes from 90 to nearly 100 percent.

Watch What You Say

There are two broad types of advertising—brand and item. Brand advertising is designed to raise awareness or show the uniqueness of a company or product, usually without mentioning the price. An example of this is a television commercial for a car that shows the vehicle, but doesn't mention price. This commercial shows the personality of the brand and the model in an effort to position the car in consumers' minds.

The preprints loaded into your Sunday newspaper are a prime example of item advertising. There are dozens and dozens of pages filled with pictures of merchandise sold either at full price or on sale. Item advertising is designed to entice you to shop for specific merchandise and, in addition to preprints, is used in catalogs, direct marketing postcards, as well as television.

Most companies do both brand and item advertising, sometimes without realizing it. One of the best examples is department stores. The physical stores themselves are their brand advertising. The facilities are usually gorgeous, with marble floors, fancy display cases, and designer clothes. Their item advertising, which is mostly price-based and filled with money-saving offers and promotions, completely contradicts the upscale image of the stores. When customers get mixed messages, they get confused. And when they get confused they take their business to a place where they know what they're going to get. That's why the average income from shoppers in department stores has been declining steadily for the past fifteen years. And that's why department store profits have been declining just as steadily.

Contrast that with Nordstrom, which has very upscale stores and runs only one or two sales per year and has revenues per square foot that are nearly twice as high as traditional department stores. Nordstrom also has an entirely different set of stores called Nordstrom Rack, which stock closeouts and other discounted items, and look much more industrial. That way, people who can't generally afford to shop at a regular Nordstrom store can still come home with a Nordstrom bag and feel a little more prosperous.

Know Thyself, or at Least Thy Sweet Spot

Another major advertising blunder companies make is losing track of their sweet spot and where they are in the market. And if the companies don't know where they are, how can their customers?

My company was working with a large department store chain and had the opportunity to review their entire advertising program. Like most department stores, my client had a sixteen-week ad cycle, which meant they initially started planning an ad sixteen weeks before it actually ran. That's all fairly standard stuff. But what was remarkable was that every Monday, the management team would get together in a conference room and review the ads that other companies had run the weekend before. Then they'd tear apart their own ads for the coming weeks to respond to the competition. Sometimes they'd have to redo their ads ten or twelve times before publishing them.

The company had no strategy and direction. They'd forgotten about their sweet spot and spent all their energy being reactive rather than proactive, responding to other companies that may or may not have been actual competitors. They had no idea whether those "competitive" ads were successful for the companies that ran them, let alone whether they'd be successful for my client. Worse yet, very often the perceived competitors' core customer was different than the must-have customer my client needed to be successful.

Reach Out and Touch Someone.
Well, Not Just Anyone . . .

Now that you're confident in knowing what your sweet spot is and who your core and must-have customers are, your next task is to figure out how to reach them. And that's a lot harder than it used to be. Back in the 1960s, advertisers could reach as many as 90 percent of American households by running a prime-time ad on the three networks: ABC, CBS, and NBC. Today, to reach the same group, you'd have to run your ad on over one hundred channels.

There are all sorts of clever ways to reach people besides television, and I'll talk about some of them later on in this chapter. But even if you had the budget to do what it takes to reach everyone in the country (or your neighborhood, county, state, or even the world), it would be a huge mistake to try. While you might be able to get your ad into 90 percent of U.S. households, there's no guarantee that anyone will actually pay any attention to it. In fact, I can guarantee you that most people won't.

The average American is subjected to thousands of

advertising messages every day. Don't believe me? Count 'em for yourself. I've tried a few times but got up into the hundreds and lost count before I'd even left the house. There are the obvious ads on TV and radio, in newspapers, on billboards, on the tops of taxis, spam e-mail, and all the Internet pop-ups and banners. But there are many, many more subtle ads: the store signs you pass on your way to work, corporate logos on people's clothing, slogans on trucks and cars, product placements in movies, and, of course, the brand names emblazoned on every single thing you look at or touch. Tuning out advertising has become an act of self-defense.

According to a recent study by Yankelovich Partners, 65 percent of U.S. consumers feel that they're being constantly bombarded by ad messages. Fifty-nine percent feel that most ads have little or no relevance to them, and 69 percent said they'd be interested in products or services that would stop unwanted marketing. Is it any wonder that people toss out newspaper inserts without reading them, delete unwanted e-mail without opening it, and zap commercials on TiVo, or at least take advantage of the break to go to the bathroom?

What About Slogans?

Every year businesses, large and small, from all over the world, pay ad agencies millions (maybe billions) of dollars trying to come up with brand-building slogans. Unfortunately, despite the investment, most Americans are unable to identify even the most familiar slogans, according to a 2004 survey by Atlanta-based brand strategy company Emergence.

From a list of twenty-five of America's best-known brands, including GE, Budweiser, Chrysler, Wal-Mart, and Coca-Cola, only three (Allstate's "You're in good hands," State Farm's "Like a good neighbor," and Wal-Mart's "Always low prices. Always") were recognized by over half of those surveyed. Fewer than half of the slogans were recognized by more than 5 *percent* of the population, and 20 percent were recognized by 1 percent or less. Some of the biggest losers were Kmart ("Right here, right now"), Staples ("That was easy"), and Wendy's ("It's better here").

Many companies know they're wasting their money, but they just can't seem to stop themselves. At the time the 2004 survey was done, six of the twenty-three slogans from 2003 had already been dumped.

As an advertiser, the thought that no one knows your slogan or that no one's paying attention to your advertising can be pretty scary. But there is a solution.

Welcome to Relevance

Have you ever bought something that you thought was fairly unique and then been surprised at how, all of a sudden, that same product seems to be everywhere? You've just had a brush with relevance. When something touches you in some way or seems to satisfy a need, you pay attention to it. But if you have no need for it, it becomes background noise. A good example of this might be disposable diapers. If you're the parent of a child under three, a newspaper or magazine coupon from Huggies will catch your eye. If your children are grown or you don't have any, you'll turn the page and not even notice the coupon.

The million-dollar question is, How do I make my advertising relevant? A thorough discussion of this topic would fill up several volumes, but I can sum it up fairly easily. Think of it this way: Your advertising is essentially an answer to your must-have customer's question, What's in it for me? You have to give them a reason to buy from you instead of from someone else. And the way you do that is to get back to the shared values we talked about in Chapter 1. They're the attributes that make your product or service different, the attributes that your core and must-have customers demand. And only your company can deliver them!

Getting Your Message Out There

Step one, put down your shotgun and pick up a rifle. The shotgun approach to advertising is to blast the same message out to everyone everywhere and hope people buy what you're selling. The rifle approach involves very carefully targeting the people you want to reach—and who want to be reached by you—with a message that's relevant and meaningful to them.

Step two, deliver the message. The medium or media you use—television, radio, newspapers, or something else—will depend on your budget, the kind of business you're in, how your must-have customers like to be approached, and, most important, on your own creativity. Consumers buy milk every week, toothpaste every other month, tires every three years, and a washer and dryer every twelve. The media strategy needs to match the product. Suffice it to say, though, that the opportunities are limitless.

Most big advertisers have relied on television for the bulk of their advertising. But more and more companies are realizing that television doesn't provide enough bang for the buck. In 2004, Deutsche Bank did an in-depth study of twenty-three household, personal care, food, and beverage brands in the U.S. to determine the effectiveness of their television advertising. They found that TV ads almost always led to incremental increases in sales volume. However—and this is a very big however—only 18 percent of the ads generated a positive financial return. Over the longer term, things got a little better, with 45 percent of ads producing a positive return. But that leaves 55 percent of ads with a negative return. I guess that shows that even though people complain about it, bombarding them with advertising actually works, about half the time. You'd have a better chance of making money by taking your entire advertising budget to Las Vegas and betting it all on red.

A number of major advertisers have already started putting their TV shotguns away. McDonald's, for example, now spends about one-third of its ad budget on television, down from two-thirds less than a decade ago. The money that used to go for TV now pays for much more targeted, nontraditional ads. McDonald's reaches young men by advertising on Foot Locker's in-store video network. They reach young women by advertising in women's magazines and Web sites. They reach Hispanics by sponsoring closed-circuit sports programs in bars, and they reach African Americans through ads in *Upscale,* a magazine that's distributed to African-American barber shops.

Procter & Gamble, the world's biggest advertiser, used to do about 90 percent of its advertising on television. Now it's about 25 percent, and Coca-Cola is shifting some of its ad budget from TV to what they're calling "experience-based, access-driven marketing." The company's new Web site, cokemusic.com, is a great example. Visitors can play games, check out Coke-related merchandise, create their own blogs, and even download music. The site has become incredibly popular with its target market: teens.

But television advertising is far from dead, and relevant ads can be—and are—very successful. In 2000, Dell introduced a series of spots with Steven, a hip young guy who brought us the phrase, "Dude, you're getting a Dell!" The ads were aimed at young home PC users. During the time that the Steven ads were running, Dell's sales increased 16 percent. In 2002, Dell replaced Steven (after the actor who played him was busted on drug charges) with ads featuring a group of "eager interns." These spots were targeting businesses or educational institutions (which account for 70 to 80 percent of the company's revenues) instead of the home users. In the first quarter after the intern ads began, Dell's sales jumped 25 percent. And even the rather gloomy Deutsche Bank study found that some brands, including Gatorade, Tide, and Bud Light, all had positive returns on their TV advertising investment.

Let's take a brief look at some other ways of delivering relevant advertising messages.

• **The Internet.** Although it accounts for a relatively small percentage of overall ad spending, that percentage is growing fast. From 2003 to 2004, Internet ad spending was up 31.5 percent, according to PriceWaterhouseCoopers. Broadcast TV spending was up only 10 percent, and the industry in general was up only 7.4 percent. The year 2004 was also the first time that Internet ad spending exceeded year 2000 levels, just before the dot-com implosion. Internet advertising will only get more popular as more people go online to research products before buying. About 70 percent of American new car buyers do research and get price quotes online. The Internet's amazing information-gathering potential makes it possible to target ads almost down to a single individual. Amazon.com is a master at this. If you've ever bought anything from them, you've probably received an e-mail at some time, saying, "Since you recently bought a book on ABC, we thought you might be interested in one on DBF." Brilliant. But more important, relevant.

• **Radio.** According to a 2005 study done by the Radio Ad Effectiveness Lab, radio advertising is 49 percent more effective than television advertising. For one thing, it's a lot cheaper. And radio stations tend to attract homogeneous audiences, which makes targeting your core and must-have customers much easier. Also, consumer surveys have found that fewer than one in four radio listeners find advertising annoying, compared to well over half for television.

• **Print (magazines and newspapers).** A number of studies have shown that print ads are even more effective than radio (only about 10 percent of readers say they find print ads annoying). Yes, many, such as *Time* and *Newsweek,* cast a wide net. But there are hundreds that have a clearly defined targeted group that advertisers can reach. Think *Cosmopolitan, Men's Health, The AARP Bulletin, Teen People, Forbes, Dog Lover,* and so on.

• **Viral marketing.** Not that long ago, word-of-mouth advertising was something that just happened—companies had very little control over it. After a while, they figured out that they could plant stories and generate a little buzz in their own favor. In 2001, Procter

& Gamble took viral marketing to a whole new level. They created an organization called Tremor, which is a group of almost 300,000 "influential" thirteen to nineteen-year-olds. P&G gives the kids free samples, CDs, and movie passes and gently asks that the kids share them with their friends.

Tremor also does work for quite a few non-P&G clients, including some of the biggest brands in the world. It helped Pringles introduce a new flavor, Valvoline, to get the word out about a new motor oil, DreamWorks pick a logo for a film, Sony introduce an alternative to Apple's iPod, and Shamrock Farms launch a new chocolate drink.

• **Tryvertising.** The notion that putting a product in a prospective customer's hands leads to sales has been around for decades—perfumed pages in magazines, soap samples delivered with your Sunday paper, free product trials, and more recently, there are dozens of Web sites that do nothing but send out free samples. But as with viral marketing, tryvertising is reaching new heights. Porsche and Mercedes-Benz have partnered with high-end hotels to let well-heeled guests try out—for free—the latest models. On the other end of the scale, IKEA has furnished the rooms in a number of budget hotels. Starbucks installs free coffee machines in offices around the country. Even some online dating Web sites are offering free trials, hoping that a couple of nice dates will entice you to sign up for a membership.

• **Targeted coupons.** This is one of the most focused types of advertising. Every time I go to the grocery store, I pick up a few containers of the store-brand yogurt. And along with my receipt, the checker always hands me a custom-printed coupon for Yoplait. The same kind of thing happens with all sorts of other products. Buy one brand and you get a coupon for a competitor's.

This is by no means an exhaustive list. With the possible exception of television, any or all of these approaches are within just about any company's budget. But whichever option(s) you go with, choose wisely and do plenty of research. For example, with magazine and newspaper advertising, circulation figures and market niche are important, but not everything. A 2004 paper by B-school professors Bobby J. Calder and Edward C. Malthouse reported that people who find the stories in a magazine or newspaper more absorbing also have more positive reactions to the advertising in the magazine. That means that while advertising your line of fishing lures in *Bass Fisherman* might be a great idea, there might be certain issues that will be more engaging to readers. And that's where you want to be.

Okay, Let's Talk Money

Advertising is traditionally sold on a CPM basis, meaning X dollars for every thousand people theoretically reached. Typically, the larger the audience, the lower the CPM. That, in a nutshell, has caused countless companies to waste immeasurable amounts of money.

Think back to the example I gave earlier of Ultimate Electronics. On a CPM basis, Ultimate didn't pay very much for their Denver *Post* ads. But as we saw, while they may have reached thousands of eyeballs, the ads were completely irrelevant to the vast majority of readers.

By itself, CPM is a useless calculation. What you really want is CPM–MHC (cost per thousand–must-have customers). Of course, no ad agency is going to give you a CPM–MHC quote, and if you ask for one they'll look at you as though you'd just arrived from Pluto. So you'll probably have to make the calculation yourself.

There were dozens of ways that Ultimate could have reached its must-have customers. Besides redoing the ads to emphasize their market position, they could have advertised in high-end stereo magazines, or bought lists of high-income people or people who recently bought BMWs, and so on. Yes, those lists would have been pretty expensive on a traditional CPM basis, but on a CPM–MHC basis, they would have been a bargain, since Ultimate's must-have customers would have actually seen the ads.

Having said all that, what's even more important than cost per thousand–must-have customers is *results* per thousand.

Measuring Effectiveness

There's funny advertising, there's dramatic advertising, there's memorable advertising, but is there effective advertising? Well, every week *USA Today* and Harris Interactive produce the AdTrack Index, which rates major advertising campaigns based on how effective consumers think the ads are. While AdTrack results make for interesting reading, they're basically useless. To start with, AdTrack asks the wrong people. Rather than talk to each advertiser's must-have customers, they use a randomly selected group of people to rate the ads. As a result, people without driver's licenses are voting on car ads and vegetarians are voting on hamburger ads. You see what I mean.

Second, the word "effective" can be very slippery. Effective in increasing brand awareness? Effective in increasing sales? AdTrack does ask consumers how effective they think the ads would be in helping sell the product, which is a step in the right direction. But it doesn't ask whether or not the ads actually *generated any sales.*

There are only three measures of advertising effectiveness.

1. Did my core customers increase their spending with my company after seeing my advertising?
2. Did any must-have customers start doing business with us after seeing the advertising?
3. Did the ads generate a net profit?

Each of these three factors can—and must—be measured accurately. Unfortunately, too many CEOs, marketing managers, and ad execs don't believe that, and they don't even try. And most of those who do believe that advertising effectiveness can be measured end up measuring the wrong things.

Call your ad agency or your VP of marketing and announce that you want to start measuring the three factors the way I'm suggesting, and you'll probably hear all sorts of excuses and meaningful-sounding phrases. "Don't worry about the results, we're gaining 'share of mind,'" is a favorite of many agencies. Sounds clever, but I've never seen a company survive on share of mind. What you really want is share of wallet from your core customers. One common alternative to the share-of-mind answer is "we're increasing consumer awareness." No question, customer awareness is nice—people can't buy your product or service unless they're aware of it. Awareness by itself, however, isn't worth much. In the 2004 presidential election, *everyone* was aware of John Kerry. He lost. And huge levels of awareness didn't do much to keep Kmart, Montgomery Ward, and dozens of other major corporations from going belly up.

Another phrase you're likely to hear is "the cumulative effect of multiple media." Sounds like it should work, doesn't it? Problem is that it never does. If you run an ad, whether print, television, radio, or whatever, and you can't measure results over a reasonable period of time, the advertising is not working. Layering one medium on top of another may prove that the second medium works, but it doesn't improve the first.

And my all-time favorite is, "This creative is breakthrough. Our agency won an award!" Well, congratulations. But your agency's award isn't going to do you much good the next time you miss your earnings estimate.

Remember the Energizer Bunny, the California Raisins, and the Taco Bell Chihuahua? These are just a few examples of advertising that was incredibly successful in every area except where it really mattered: generating profits.

Energizer has used the bunny in more than fifty ads and has spent tens of millions of dollars over the past ten years making him into a household name. They've been very successful—just about everyone loves that little guy. Unfortunately for Energizer, 40 percent of consumers believe that the bunny is the mascot for Duracell.

The California Raisin Advisory Board's California Raisins were a hit from the first time they belted out "I Heard It Through the Grapevine." People loved them, talked about them, and even bought raisin dolls for their kids and themselves, but they didn't buy raisins. Four years into the campaign, sales were lower than they had been before the ads started.

Taco Bell introduced the Chihuahua in 1997, and in 1998 sales were up 3 percent. Like the Energizer Bunny and the California Raisins, everyone knew the

Chihuahua. But by 1999, Taco Bell's same-store sales were down 6 percent. Eventually, the company stopped polishing the glass on its advertising award trophy case and retired the Chihuahua to the doghouse.

Getting Your Money's Worth

Despite what you might hear from ad execs, there are many ways to measure the return on your advertising spending. Over the course of two decades of analyzing advertising effectiveness, I've seen a number of tracking systems with very sophisticated algorithms that attempt to account for every eventuality. But I've yet to see one that works well, or that a company has used for more than a few months.

So my company created a more basic—and far more successful—system that we call Plus Over Normal. It works like this: Every ad is benchmarked against the normal business baseline. The lift from the ad in sales dollars, units, and gross margin dollars can then be evaluated.

A word of warning: It's essential that you track sales *and* margins. From our analysis using the Plus-Over-Normal model, we've discovered that it's quite possible to increase or maintain sales levels while actually decreasing profits. For example, items can be put on sale, but if unit sales stay flat, margins drop by whatever the price reduction was times the number of units sold. Now, you might think this type of performance is unusual. However, the unfortunate fact is that based on a number of analyses we have completed, negative results based on faulty advertising are more the norm than the exception. Remember those Sunday newspaper inserts we talked about earlier? We have been hard-pressed to find one that provides a consistent, positive return on investment.

I suggest that you use a variety of ways to evaluate your advertising. Here are a few methods that work extremely well.

- **Code each ad.** You see this kind of thing all the time. Have you ever seen commercials that tell you to call the 800 number and ask for Operator

123, or mail-in coupons that are addressed to Department 456? Those are internal codes that let the advertiser know which of its ads are generating what response. You can slice these results as finely as you want. Retail stores, for example, tend to measure sales volume per square foot. My friend who ran the Home Decorators Collection catalog knew his profitability down to the tenth of a page—that's how many products usually fit on one page.

- **Do single-item ads.** After establishing the baseline for a particular product, run an ad for it, but don't do any other promotion.

- **Stop advertising.** If you're running a campaign and don't have a baseline, the only way to establish one is to stop all advertising in all or some of your markets and see what happens to your numbers. Several of my clients have done this and have been horrified to find that their sales didn't change at all. And when you factor in the cost of the ads, they were actually better off not running them at all.

- **If your advertising isn't working, find out why.** The most effective way to determine why advertising doesn't work is to, yep, you guessed it, ask your core and must-have customers. You'll want to pose questions like these:

- Have you seen or heard any advertising for (the name of your business category) in the past thirty days?
- Where did you see or hear the advertising?
- Who was the advertising for?
- Did the advertising cause you to seek more information or actually purchase the product?
- Did you purchase any additional products?

What's Wrong with Ad Agencies?

After reading this chapter and the case studies I've described, you may be asking yourself, What's wrong with ad agencies? In many ways, the answer is nothing. Most ad agencies are not experts in your business, they are experts in advertising. They know about creative, production, and media, but they don't know about your unique strategy, positioning, desired sweet spot, or most importantly, your core and must-have customers. Ultimately, you—and not your agency—are responsible for your business and its results. If the creative and media are not specifically targeted to the customers you need for sustained profitable growth, it's your responsibility to say NO! It's not always easy, but your business is on the line, not the agency's.

The Must-Have Audit

Most businesspeople associate the word "audit" with accounting or the SEC or compliance issues or annual reports that (hopefully) demonstrate that the company is reporting accurate information about its financial well-being. And when it comes to financial audits, that's all true.

Now, don't get me wrong: I have nothing against financial audits—it's certainly important to know that all the beans were put into the right pots and that everything that happened in the previous twelve months was properly accounted for. But there's a limit to the usefulness of analyzing the past and knowing that your accounting department is doing what it's supposed to be doing.

For that reason, I want to propose a completely different kind of audit, one that looks at the future rather than the past. My proposed audit—let's call it the "must-have audit"—is all about creating continuous improvement, getting better every day, every week, every month, and every year. Instead of a snapshot of your company at a specific moment in time, the must-have audit is a constantly evolving work in progress.

A successful must-have audit is designed to track how well you understand who your core and must-have customers are, what their rules are, and how they position your business. Here are some of the questions you'll need to ask yourself:

- At what rate are we turning must-have customers into core customers?
- How have our must-have customers improved their opinion of our company or brand?
- How have they redefined our competition?

- Have we carved out a sweet spot and are we dominating it?
- Are our core customers spending more or less with our company?
- Are we reducing the percentage of customers who are opportunistic?
- Are we getting better at hiring the right people for our company and putting them in the right jobs?
- Are we reducing must-have employee turnover?
- Are we listening to what our employees are telling us about how to improve our business?
- Is our advertising becoming more effective with our core and must-have customers?
- Can they accurately repeat the message we're sending to them?

Every answer should be quantifiable and tracked. Remember the old management axiom, You can only manage what you can measure. Sound complicated? It can be, but if you've been paying attention to the first seven chapters of this book, you have a good, solid base to build from.

The management review of the must-have audit findings can be done in a series of regularly scheduled, on-site meetings or an annual two- or three-day off-site meeting. Now, rather than debating opinions, you can thoughtfully discuss facts and effectively plan the future. You can use an in-house facilitator to conduct the sessions or hire a qualified consultant to guide the review. Whichever route you decide to go, everyone involved needs to be focused on the task at hand. And you need to have the most recent research, information, and reports to accurately assess whether what you've been doing so far has been moving your company in a positive direction or not. By reviewing the answers to the above questions, you'll have a much better picture of what the future will bring.

With a little luck, your must-have audit will show that you've set your company on a steady, forward path and that all you need is a little tweaking to optimize your results. You know your competition, you've created a sweet spot that would-be competitors can't touch, you know your customers' rules, and so on. In short, you can confidently answer yes to all the questions outlined above. You'll be able to implement plans for your company built on this information and you'll have a significant competitive advantage that will be difficult to overcome. You'll also provide reassurance to your organization and its shareholders that your company, division, or business unit has a profitable and bright future.

If you're not quite that lucky, the must-have audit will reveal exactly what you're doing wrong and will highlight the specific problem areas you'll need to correct. If this happens, don't feel bad—it's a rare company that doesn't identify at least a few areas that demand some significant improvement. You'll need to analyze the data you've gathered (or gather some if you haven't already), and adjust your strategy so you can achieve your goal of building a profitable company.

Again, as I mentioned earlier, the must-have audit is a process that never ends. Companies committed to continuous improvement realize that standing still is actually sliding backwards. Change never stops. Competition never stops. Your customers' rules don't remain the same. So make your must-have audits an ongoing part of running your business. You'll be glad you did.

ACKNOWLEDGMENTS

Now for the most challenging chapter in the book. I have attempted to write this chapter one hundred times in my head. While my name appears in large type on the cover, there are many people responsible for the existence of this book. After much thought I decided the most appropriate way to thank people would be based upon the amount of time I have known them and the influence they have had on my life and learning.

It is truly appropriate for me to first thank my incredible wife of forty years, Elly. The simple truth is

Elly's name should have appeared on the cover. Elly motivated me to write the book, single-handedly did all of the research, wrote the first draft, and most important, kept me on track. The reality is, no Elly, no book.

It is appropriate that the next person I thank, the person with the second-longest tenure in my life, is Jim Posner. Jim has been the greatest contributor to my business education, my mentor and best friend for almost thirty years. Jim introduced me to consumer research and Must-Have Customer 101. He has been and continues to be my teacher.

Most people are not fortunate enough to have one mentor. I was blessed with two. My second mentor, Don Clifton, taught me the most important lesson of my business career—recognize the strengths of people, build from those strengths, and don't destroy people by trying to fix their weaknesses. Don was a builder of people and only saw the good. Don would have found only the strengths of this book and none of the weaknesses. I regret that Don is not with us to read this book.

Not long after I met Don, I met Marcus Buckingham. Marcus and I were at Gallup at the same time, but rarely worked together. When I decided to write the book, Marcus was already a best-selling author. After one call he was willing to help and provided much-needed advice. Marcus has provided ideas, direction, and has been a true friend.

The next group to enter my life and make this book a reality were my book team of Lee and Donna Synnott, Jim Levine, Armin Brott, and Mac Talley. This is the level of team you take to the Super Bowl. Lee and Donna Synnott are two of the finest people I have ever met. Whether it's helping a friend write and market a book or giving back to their community, nothing is too much for Lee and Donna.

Jim Levine was the first person in the book industry to express confidence in this project and a first-time author. I hope he was right.

Jim introduced us to Armin Brott, and this project took a turn in the right direction. We knew what we wanted to say, but Armin knew how to say it. He not only made the concepts readable and interesting, he brought a new, fresh, and often better perspective to some of them.

The final member of the book team is Truman

"Mac" Talley, our editor. When you look in the dictionary under *wisdom* you'll find a picture of Mac. Every conversation with Mac is a learning experience. He has provided the short course to teach me what I didn't know about the publishing business.

I want to thank those people who read various versions of the book and gave us constructive feedback—Bill and Vicki Crouch, Andie Gordman, Jay Gordman, Robert Hafner, Nancy Karklins, and Donna Schultz.

I would have not been able to write this book without the incredible breadth of experiences I've had the past fifteen years, working for a remarkable group of clients. I genuinely appreciate the opportunities they have given me to explore unique and interesting challenges in so many industries. It was these experiences that helped me to understand the power and importance of the Must-Have Customer.

My final note of appreciation goes to my wonderful family—Andie, Brandon, Lindsey, Jay, Allison, Spencer, and Powder. It is remarkable that we all like to be together and party together. The best week of the year is our out-of-control family ski week—twelve hours of laughter every day that is exhilarating and exhausting.

INDEX

INDEX